At the mouth of the tunnel
N.L.&M. Co. Cal.

GHOST TOWNS OF NORTHERN CALIFORNIA

Your Guide to Ghost Towns
and Historic Mining Camps

Text by Philip Varney
Photographs by
John and Susan Drew

Voyageur Press

*A Pictorial
Discovery Guide*

Text copyright © 2001 by Philip Varney
Photographs copyright © 2001 by John and Susan Drew, except as noted

Edited by Amy Rost-Holtz
Designed by Andrea Rud
Jacket designed by Maria Friedrich
Map illustrations by Mary Firth
Printed in Hong Kong

First hardcover edition:
01   02   03   04   05   5   4   3   2   1
First softcover edition:
01   02   03   04   05   5   4   3   2   1

Library of Congress Cataloging-in-Publication Data available

ISBN 0-89658-444-5 (hardcover)
ISBN 0-89658-442-9 (softcover)

Distributed in Canada by Raincoast Books, 9050 Shaughnessy Street, Vancouver, B.C. V6P 6E5

Published by Voyageur Press, Inc.
123 North Second Street, P.O. Box 338, Stillwater, MN 55082 U.S.A.
651-430-2210, fax 651-430-2211
books@voyageurpress.com
www.voyageurpress.com

On the frontispiece, top: *Miners riding mule-drawn ore cars prepare to enter the New Idria's Quicksilver Mine's No. 10 Tunnel in a photo dating from about 1910. (Courtesy of the California History Room, California State Library, Sacramento)*
Bottom: *The entrance to the long-closed machine shop at the Empire Mine State Park has an ore car ready for "repair."*

Title page, main photo: *The Chemung Mine commands a panoramic view of the snow-tipped Sierra Nevada.*

Title page, inset photo: *The barbershop in Columbia began serving patrons in 1865. In the rear of the building, miners could bathe in tubs.*

DEDICATION

To my daughter, Janet Varney—a San Franciscan, despite her Arizona desert roots.
And in loving memory of Laura Durgin and Jean Ten Broeck.

Placer gold rests in the pan of a balance scale.

CONTENTS

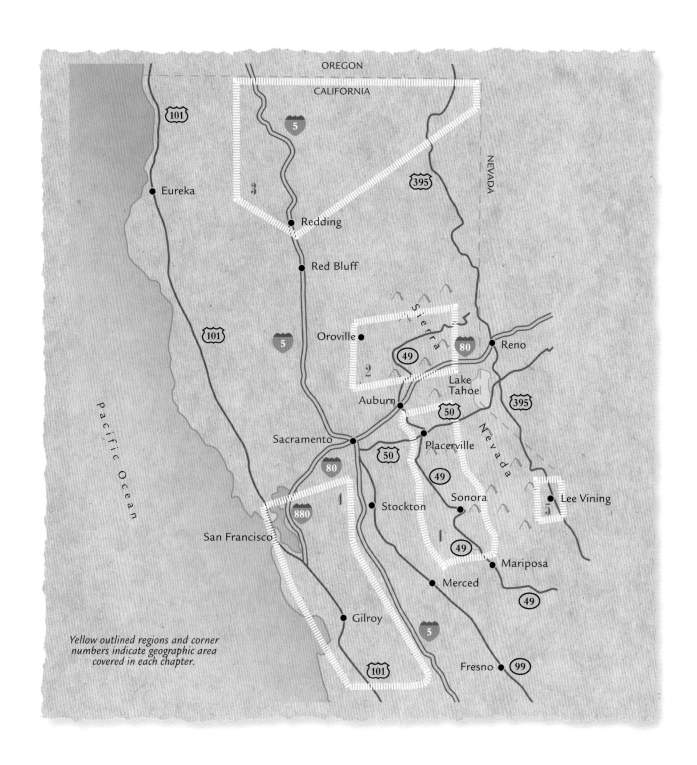

Yellow outlined regions and corner
numbers indicate geographic area
covered in each chapter.

TO THE READER

Ghost Towns of Northern California is intended for people who seek the unusual, enjoy history, and savor solitude. Some of the destinations in this book will be unfamiliar to most Californians, like out-of-the-way Campo Seco, New Idria, and Bennettville. Other sites attract thousands of visitors annually, such as Coloma, Columbia, and Bodie. Chasing down ghost towns and mining camps in this book will take you from sea level to more than 10,000 feet elevation. You will view some of the West's loveliest rivers and grandest mountaintops. In the process, I hope you will see California as you have never seen it before. That certainly happened to me.

I was a ghost town hunter long before I became a ghost town writer. I had been prowling California's back roads in search of the forgotten since 1974. My third ghost town book, published in 1990, covered California from the Mexican border to Death Valley and Inyo County. This, my sixth book on ghost towns, extends from New Idria, in the hills southwest of Fresno, ventures through the '49er Gold Rush Country, makes a surprising stop in San Francisco Bay, and proceeds to the northern and eastern reaches of California.

My first ghost town book was written as a result of my frustration with the way such books are generally organized. I wanted a completely practical, informative guide that would give me everything I needed next to me on the seat of my truck. That first book's success has led to five more, including this one.

This volume, like my others, arranges towns geographically, so you can visit places in logical groups, beginning with Coloma, where the Gold Rush began, and ending with the ghosts of the Eastern Sierra, which sit in some of California's most captivating scenery.

Each chapter features a map of the area, a history of each town, specific directions to each site, and recommendations when necessary for vehicle requirements. For example, some towns are adjacent to an interstate, while others require a high-clearance vehicle (however, I never had to use four-wheel drive for this book). For two sites, my photographer partners and I left our truck behind and hiked. For two other sites, I used a mountain bike to excellent advantage.

Most towns in this book fall into the rather broad category of "mining camps." Few entries are true ghost towns. By my definition, a ghost town has two characteristics: The population has decreased markedly, and the initial reason for its settlement (in northern California, usually gold) no longer keeps people there. A ghost town, then, can be completely deserted, like Masonic; it can have a few residents, like Smartville; or it can have genuine signs of vitality, like many of the sites in chapters one and two.

But it cannot have too much vitality. Visitors to Gold Rush Country may wonder why I have not included some important towns along Highway 49, like Auburn, Placerville, and Sonora, which were definitely historically significant. Quite simply, if a town seemed "buried under modernity," as author-historian Richard Dillon put it, I omitted it. For example, although Placerville has some lovely downtown buildings, the twentieth century has rather overwhelmed the nineteenth.

I had mixed feelings about smaller towns like Sutter Creek and Jamestown. They weren't quite so obviously up-to-date, and both feature attractive business districts and residences, but they still seemed on the whole to be too, well, *bustling* for my taste. Since you will be traveling through many of these towns on your way to others, explore them on your own.

At the other extreme, people living in sleepy places like Fort Bidwell, La Grange, and Dutch Flat may be offended about inclusion in a "ghost town" book. But their towns have "ghost town" indicators: In each case, their population has dropped precipitously, and once-

Above: *Only the front wall remains of Volcano's Clute Building and the Kelly and Symonds Emporium.*

prosperous businesses have closed. In each of the three towns, the historic school has no students.

There must, however, be something significant remaining for a town to be included in this book. There are 59 mining camps and ghost towns in this volume, but I also visited and eliminated 104 other sites, including 48 in chapter one alone, most because so little of historic importance remained.

Although I had seen most of these towns many times, my photographers and I visited or revisited every site in 1999 or 2000. The color photographs in this book, with the exception of Bodie, were all taken within that same time period. The book's emphasis is on what remains at a town, not what was there in its heyday. I describe what to look for at each site, and, with important places such as Coloma, Murphys, and Weaverville, I suggest walking and driving tours.

Almost every town has a cemetery, even if it has little else. Some of my most enjoyable but poignant moments have come while walking around graveyards, since emotions are often laid bare on tombstones. To read the grief of parents in the epitaphs of their children is to see the West in absolutely personal terms. History comes tragically alive in cemeteries.

I also make recommendations about attractions such as museums, mine tours, and mill tours. To see them all would be somewhat repetitious, so when such attractions come up, I give advice based on my experiences at other museums and tours. Incidentally, I paid for all attractions, and guides knew me only as another tourist. Occasionally, I suggest phoning ahead for information and reservations, such as with Alcatraz and Bodie. As phone numbers and especially area codes are subject to change, I have not included them in this book. However, all the appropriate phone numbers are available in the American Automobile Association's (AAA) tour books of California.

As you visit the places in this book, please remember that ghost towns are extremely fragile. Leave a site as you found it. I have seen many items on the back roads that tempted me, but I have no collection of artifacts. If you must pick up something, how about a film wrapper or an aluminum can?

Inside a lovely, abandoned old home in Colorado is posted the following notice, which eloquently conveys what should be our deportment at ghost towns and mining camps:

Attention: We hope that you are enjoying looking at our heritage. The structure may last many more years for others to see and enjoy if everyone like you treads lightly and takes only memories and pictures.

Philip Varney
Tucson

Bodie's Cameron House displays common household items and an empty picture frame only slightly out of true.

"GOLD! GOLD! GOLD FROM THE AMERICAN RIVER!"

When James Marshall found gold in California's American River on January 24, 1848, he set into motion one of the most incredible economic and social upheavals in history. When he made his find, California was still a part of Mexico. Nine days later, Mexico ceded to the United States a vast territory west from Texas and north to Oregon. In doing so, Mexico gave up, unknowingly, the most astonishing concentration of gold the world has ever seen.

Originally Marshall's find was viewed with skepticism: A San Francisco newspaper in May 1848 scoffed, "A few fools have hurried to the [American River], but you may be sure there is nothing in it."

A few days later, however, storekeeper Sam Brannan, who had been to the area of Marshall's discovery, paraded through San Francisco with a bottle full of gold dust, exclaiming, "Gold! Gold! Gold from the American River!" The rush was on, and San Francisco practically emptied, its citizens heading to the gold fields—and conveniently stopping by Brannan's store, full of supplies, along the way (Brannan would, as a result, become one of California's wealthiest men). Another of the city's newspapers complained a few days later that "the field is left half planted, the house half built, and everything neglected but the manufacture of shovels and pick axes." San Francisco's harbor eventually was clogged with rotting, crewless ships.

In 1848, only 400 people immigrated to California. During the following year, with word of Marshall's discovery trumpeted around the world, an astounding 90,000 people descended upon the area. Author J. S. Holliday states that California "would be transformed from obscurity to world prominence;... from a society of neighbors and families to one of strangers and transients; from an ox-cart economy based on hides and tallow to a complex economy based on gold mining."

Gold seekers swarmed across the nation on the early pioneer routes that had opened the West, like the Oregon and Santa Fe trails. Some attempted short cuts across infamous Death Valley, while others took a southern route that crossed arid sections of Arizona and Mexico. The average successful trip took about a hundred days and covered 2,000 miles.

Those who could afford the passage often opted for sea travel. A 15,000-mile journey from New York to San Francisco around Cape Horn took from five to eight months, but those willing to brave the dangers of the jungle could cross the isthmus of Nicaragua or Panama and shorten the sea voyage to six to eight weeks.

Whatever route they used, the Argonauts came and came. Between 1848 and 1860, California's population exploded from 14,000 to 300,000. In the early days of the rush, the population was almost exclusively male. One lad in Nevada City inscribed in his diary, "Got nearer to a female this evening than I have been for six months. Came near fainting."

Not all the hopefuls came from the United States,

Above: *The lure of enormous riches in California is captured by the very name of the clipper ship* Eldorado. *This "clipper card" was used to advertise the ship's swift passage to potential Argonauts. (Courtesy of the California History Room, California State Library, Sacramento)*

although estimates range at more than 65 percent American. Mexicans and Chileans streamed in from the south. English, Scots, Irish, and Welsh, many of them experienced miners, came from the British Isles. Germans, French, and Scandinavians arrived. By 1852, about 25,000 Chinese had joined the throng, looking for the promised wealth of *Gum Shan*, "The Golden Mountain."

The reason for the stampede was genuine. The Mother Lode was an immense body of gold that extended down the western foothills of the Sierra Nevada for an unbelievable distance of a hundred miles. It began north of Coloma and ended near Bear Valley (an area covered in this book by chapter one).

Although the Mother Lode was the most famous, there were other extremely rich deposits found in Nevada, Placer, and Sierra counties (chapter two). A third bonanza was revealed only two months after Marshall's discovery when Major Pierson B. Reading found gold more than 200 miles north of San Francisco, leading to a separate gold rush near the Trinity and Klamath rivers (chapter three).

The size and scope of the California Gold Rush defies simple description, but it can be capsulized in two almost unimaginable facts: In a mere four years, the world's supply of gold *doubled*, and with the United States leading the way, more gold was discovered worldwide between 1850 and 1875 than in the previous 350 years combined.

Initially, gold was easily retrieved from secondary deposits in streams and along banks. The gold's size varied from small particles, known as "flour gold," to nuggets weighing as much as several pounds. Prospectors would then search upstream for the source of that water-borne gold. Those primary deposits were often so pure that gold could be extracted with a shovel—or even a spoon.

A recurring pattern developed in the quest for riches.

James Marshall stands before Sutter's nearly finished sawmill on January 19, 1848. Five days later he would discover gold in the mill's race, dramatically altering his destiny—and California's. (Courtesy of the Bancroft Library, University of California, Berkeley, BANC PIC 17175:81 ffALB)

As Henry David Thoreau said of the Argonauts, "They go to dig where they never planted, to reap where they never sowed." Prospectors were exploring everywhere that looked promising. When a discovery was made, there would be a futile attempt at secrecy. After the revelation, there would be a frantic dash to stake claims—or jump someone else's. Frequently, once the word was out, the discovery would be wildly exaggerated. Mark Twain, who witnessed the Gold Rush firsthand, once defined a mine as "a hole in the ground owned by a liar."

At the site of each new bonanza, a tent city appeared. If the deposits lasted, more permanent wooden buildings would be constructed, bringing merchants, saloonkeepers, prostitutes, and eventually a postmaster. Everyone in camp depended upon gold in one way or another. Some camps turned into full-fledged towns with solid brick buildings and signs of gentility, like newspapers and an opera house. When the gold deposits failed, however, the town would empty and the same cycle would begin again at a new "El Dorado."

The easy pickings of the Gold Rush were exhausted by the 1860s. Getting to the more difficult deposits required hardrock mining and, later, newer methods—hydraulicking and dredging. These procedures required capital investment, elaborate equipment, and an organized work force, basically ending the era of the single miner working his small claim.

Even large-scale mining eventually gave out, although some Grass Valley– and Jackson-area mines produced for decades after the Gold Rush bonanza ended about 1884.

The last two chapters of this book leave Gold Rush Country. Not all mining in California was for gold, and not all ghost towns were once mining camps. Several unusual and interesting sites stand not far from the Mother Lode near San Francisco Bay (chapter four).

Finally, during the decline of Mother Lode mining, a new strike in the 1870s brought a short but glorious life to the town of Bodie, east of the Sierra Nevada (chapter five). Bodie is a ghost town unique in the world.

To experience California's mining history, one can explore its remnants: the mining camps and ghost towns that were once abandoned in search of new wealth. The tent camps have disappeared. Visitors can walk empty hillsides where a thousand people once lived and not see a trace of their presence. The majority of wood-frame towns have vanished as well, having fallen to fire, vandalism, or salvage. Some delightful ones still exist, however, and the best are showcased throughout this book.

The communities with brick buildings, as one might expect, have generally survived the best. Chapter one's Columbia, for example, is an historic treasure. Most, however, have become the "old town" sections of modern cities that envelop their historic districts.

Why are we called to these places where so many lives have toiled and so many have been forgotten? Mystery writer Tony Hillerman, in a foreword to my New Mexico book, captured the answer: "To me, to many of my friends, to scores of thousands of Americans, these ghost towns offer a sort of touching-place with the past. We stand in their dust and try to project our imagination backward into what they were long ago. Now and then, if the mood and the weather are exactly right, we almost succeed."

Our "touching-places with the past," however, are in immediate and long-term danger. Vandals tear up floorboards hoping for a non-existent coin. Looters remove an old door with the vague notion of using it, only to discard it later. Thieves dislodge a child's headstone, heartlessly assuming no one will miss it.

Remember: These old towns are to be explored and photographed, but also protected and treasured. You must be a part of the preservation, not the destruction.

Hydraulic mining operations like this one were used at sites such as Malakoff Diggins, devastating the landscape and causing environmental disasters downstream. (Courtesy of the California History Room, California State Library, Sacramento)

Both photos: *Argonauts came from all over the world to join the Gold Rush. In these rather atypical photographs, Caucasians work alongside Chinese and African American miners. Most mining camps were highly segregated, and such cooperation was unusual. (Courtesy of the California History Room, California State Library, Sacramento)*

Chapter One

GHOSTS OF THE MOTHER LODE

Main photo: *The stone remnants of Campo Seco's Adams Express Agency Building are among the Mother Lode's most ghostly ruins.*

Inset photo: *James Marshall's statue points dramatically down to the spot on the American River where Marshall first saw gold.*

The Coloma Area

Coloma is the logical place to begin California's Gold Rush history, since it was in Coloma, on January 24, 1848, that James Marshall peered into the American River. He later recalled, "My eye was caught by something shining in the bottom of the ditch . . . it made my heart thump, for I was certain it was gold. . . . Then I saw another."

Coloma

John August Sutter, German-born of Swiss parents, came to California in 1839 and became a Mexican citizen. He received a 50,000-acre land grant and was appointed the *alcalde* (a Spanish title, embracing the duties of judge, lawyer, marshal, and mayor) for the entire Sacramento Valley.

His empire, which he called New Helvetia, featured a large adobe fort (still standing in Sacramento) that offered protection, food, and retail goods to nearby settlers. He also laid out a town called Sutterville, constructed a flour mill, and, providentially for California, sent James Marshall to the Coloma Valley, along the South Fork of the American River. There Marshall was to supervise the building of a sawmill, with Sutter and Marshall sharing the profits.

As sawmill construction neared completion, Marshall was inspecting the millrace, the channel through which the river would run to turn a wheel to power the sawmill. That is where he saw the glitter in the river, changing the course of California and utterly ruining Sutter's vision of a frontier agricultural dynasty.

As word of the gold discovery spread, Sutter's workers abandoned the unfinished sawmill and flour mill, and his field workers and other tradesmen quit to find their fortunes. The New Helvetia that Sutter had envisioned was doomed, and Coloma became not a quiet sawmill town but a camp of frenzied Argonauts.

Because there was no law enforcement, neither Sutter nor Marshall could keep squatters out, and the banks of the American River became alive with prospectors as the gold fever spread. Although Sutter tried to profit from the fabulous find, he never did. He lamented, "What a great misfortune was this sudden gold discovery for me!" He attempted to get compensation for his lost lands, but the American courts ruled that his Mexican land grants were invalid. He eventually left New Helvetia for Pennsylvania, where he was buried in 1880.

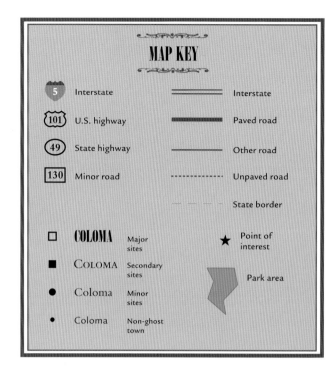

Coloma was the first Gold Rush town, but it was hardly the richest. The river's placer deposits were depleted quickly, and the town, with a population of 5,000 in 1849, was dying by 1851.

Walking and Driving Around Coloma

Most of Coloma is within Marshall Gold Discovery State Park. Begin at the visitors' center—the Gold Discovery Museum—where, in addition to paying a modest fee (for admission to the museum and park, a guide booklet, and brochures), you can see exhibits of artifacts, descriptions of gold processes, and presentations of videos.

North of the gold museum are two buildings from Coloma's Chinese community. The Man Lee Store, displays the techniques of placer mining, hardrock mining, dredging, and hydraulic mining, while the Wah Hop Store retains its original purpose as a grocery and herb store.

Across the highway is a reconstruction of Sutter's Mill. The mill is not on the original site, but a nearby trail takes you there. Adjacent to the mill is the Mormon Cabin, a 1948-built replica that features a short history of the Mormons who were in Coloma in 1848.

California Argonauts searched for placer gold like this in northern California's rivers and streams.

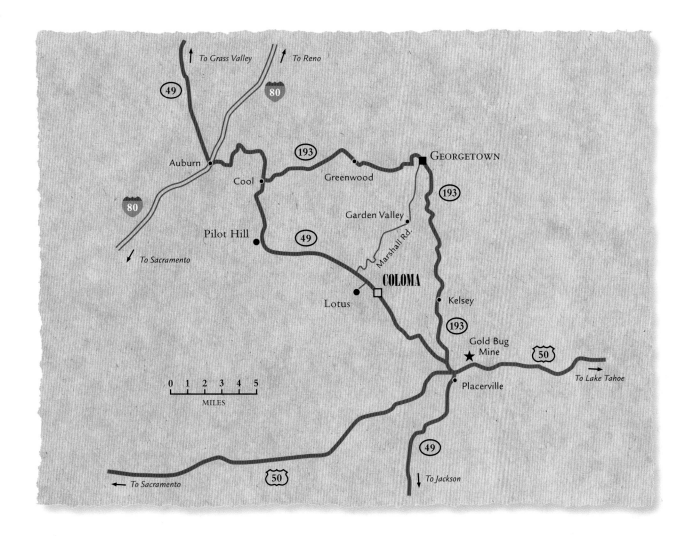

South of the sawmill on Highway 49 are several historic buildings, some open for business. Beyond those businesses is Robert Bell's Brick Store, a general merchandise and feed store that also housed the post office. Across the street but partially hidden from view is the 1854 Independent Order of Odd Fellows (I.O.O.F.) Hall.

Beyond Bell's store stands the one-room Coloma Schoolhouse.

South of the visitors' center are several buildings worth seeing, beginning with the 1857 stone block El Dorado County Jail, in use until 1862.

Southwest of the jail, on Church Street, stand—not surprisingly—two attractive churches. The first is the 1856 St. John's Catholic Church, where services were held until 1925. Behind the church is its cemetery. Across the road from that cemetery is a reconstruction of the cabin James Marshall built in 1856.

Down Church Street from St. John's is the 1856 Emmanuel Church, built jointly by Methodist and Epis-

copal congregations. James Marshall's funeral was held there in 1885. This church, like St. John's, has an iron gate, affording you a look at its simple, unadorned interior.

At the end of Church Street is Cold Springs Road, where you will find Coloma's Pioneer Cemetery just beyond the turnoff to the James Marshall Monument. A brochure at the cemetery suggests a walking tour.

Monument Road goes to the James Marshall Monument, a bronze statue erected in 1890 that shows Marshall dramatically pointing down to the spot where he found gold. Marshall, like John Sutter, never prospered from his discovery. He spent much of his life vainly searching hills and streams for another strike. He died a bitter recluse in nearby Kelsey and is buried at the monument.

When You Go

Coloma is 18 miles southeast of Auburn and 9 miles northwest of Placerville on Highway 49.

Above: *The Wah Hop Store in Coloma, built about 1858, has food items and, in the drawers left of the counter, herbs favored by Chinese Argonauts.*

Facing page: *Sutter's sawmill was reconstructed in 1968 using the methods of the 1840s, with wooden pegs and hand-adzed timbers.*

Both photos: *The 1890 Coloma Schoolhouse was brought in pieces to Coloma in 1920 from Slatington, nine miles away. The school was completely restored in July 1987, but, because of its location at a bend in the highway, it was destroyed by a runaway logging truck a mere three months later. A coalition of organizations combined their efforts to restore it again, completing the task in 1995.*

When the doors of St. John's Catholic Church are open, a wrought iron gate allows you an interior view.

Side Trip to Lotus and Pilot Hill

Consider visiting two minor sites in the Coloma area, Lotus and Pilot Hill. Following this route makes for a pleasant loop to Georgetown (see the following entry).

To reach Lotus, drive .8 of a mile north from Coloma on Highway 49 and turn left on Lotus Road and proceed .8 of a mile. Lotus, first known as Marshall, for James Marshall, then later as Uniontown, honoring California's entrance into the Union, once had 2,000 residents until placer deposits gave out. The somnolent town features the 1893 Lotus Store, Adam Lohry's General Store and home (built in 1859), and, on a hill south of town, the 1869 former Uniontown School. The Uniontown Cemetery is west of the school on Bassi Road.

Pilot Hill is 7.9 miles northwest of Coloma on Highway 49. Pilot Hill had hardrock mines to sustain it after placer deposits depleted, so it lasted longer than either Coloma or Lotus. The nearby Zantgraf Mine produced a million dollars' worth of gold in 1901. Mining continued intermittently until 1941.

At Pilot Hill stands the decaying but still imposing three-story 1862 Bayley Mansion. The once-elegant building, which has lost its wooden front porch and second-story veranda, was constructed by Alcander A. Bayley as a hotel in anticipation of the Central Pacific Railroad. When the railroad bypassed Pilot Hill by eight miles, Bayley had a mansion—by default—with an inordinate number of bedrooms. Locals dubbed the structure "Bayley's Folly."

Georgetown

Gold was found near Georgetown, the northeastern-most town in the Mother Lode, in the summer of 1849. The camp was named for miner George Phipps. By December of that year Georgetown had a population of several thousand and a nickname—"Growlersburg," because nuggets were so large they "growled" in miners' pans.

The town received its post office in 1851. The following year, fire destroyed the thriving camp. Determined to contain future fires, town fathers moved Georgetown out of a canyon and laid out main streets a hundred feet wide, along with back streets sixty feet wide. Citizens of the rebuilt town, which featured many brick structures with iron fire doors, triumphantly proclaimed Georgetown "Pride of the Mountains."

Georgetown outlasted many Gold Rush camps because it had solid primary deposits, not just placer gold. In 1866, a rich vein was discovered that yielded $50,000 in gold in two days. Five mills with a combined thirty-five stamps were still operating in 1887, and production continued after the turn of the twentieth century.

With more than 3,000 residents, Georgetown today is a livelier community than other area mining camps. Several festivals and jamborees attract throngs of visitors.

Walking and Driving Around Georgetown

If you took the Lotus and Pilot Hill side trip, the first historic part of Georgetown you will see is its picturesque Pioneer Cemetery, located on State Route 193 at Greenwood Road. Headstones of immigrants from Ireland, France, Germany, Bavaria, and Switzerland demonstrate the lure of the Gold Rush. One elaborate marker has a misspelling—"Gone to be an Angle." In addition to the Europeans buried there are natives of Ohio, New York, Vermont, and North and South Carolina.

Georgetown's business district is up the highway from the cemetery on hundred-foot-wide Main Street. The first building of note is on the southeast corner, the large, brooding, I.O.O.F. Hall, which was built in 1859 as a hotel and dance hall called the Balzar House. The architecture is rather curious, with a tall brick first story and a much shorter wooden second story. It once had a third story, which was removed in the 1890s.

In downtown Georgetown, on the northwest side of Main, stands the 1852 Wells Fargo Building; two doors west is an 1862 building that was the Civil War armory.

The former American Hotel, now the American River Inn, is up the street.

When You Go

If you took the side trip from Coloma to Lotus and Pilot Hill, go 3 miles north on Highway 49 from Pilot Hill to Cool. Go east on State Route 193, Georgetown Road, for 12 miles.

From Coloma, drive 1.3 miles north on Highway 49 to Marshall Road and turn right. Follow Marshall Road for 9 miles to Georgetown.

Standing diagonally across from Georgetown's Odd Fellows Hall is the 1864 Shannon Knox House, which was built with wood shipped around Cape Horn— to a town surrounded by a forest.

The former American Hotel is the most elegant building in Georgetown. The inn has been a hotel, rooming house, sanitarium, and private residence. The original 1863 hotel burned in 1897 and was rebuilt in 1899.

Placerville's Gold Bug Mine

Although Gold Rush Country was pockmarked with mines, surprisingly little evidence of them remains. You will see dredge tailings, hydraulicking scars, and an occasional headframe, but someone not examining the area's history could overlook mining altogether. For that reason, I recommend touring the 1888 Gold Bug Mine just outside of Placerville. The visit will be short, enjoyable, informative, and inexpensive.

You can take a self-guided tour or rent an audio cassette player. I took the cassette tour but would not do so again. The 420-foot mine tunnel itself is interesting, but I found the audio's pace too slow. The narrator, supposedly a ghost who inhabits the mine, was a bit hokey for my taste. I think children especially might become impatient. My advice: go self-guided and plan for about twenty minutes inside the mine.

The Joshua Hendy Stamp Mill, however, is reason enough to visit. The building was constructed in 1986 to cover an old eight-stamp mill already there. In addition to a close-up view of the stamp mill, you get something even better: Below the original is an electrically powered model of the same mill. People who look at shut-down mines and mills have no concept of the din when they were operating. When the model starts going, it makes a startling clatter. You look up at the huge original, which went two-and-a-half times faster, and consider how loud *it* must have been. No wonder mill workers often went deaf.

To visit the Gold Bug Mine, go to Placerville, 9 miles southeast of Coloma on Highway 49. Go east on U.S. 50 and take an immediate exit, Bedford Avenue. Go left onto Spring Street, followed by a right onto Pleasant Street. Turn left at an ensuing stop sign as Bedford rejoins Pleasant. Follow Bedford over a hill and down to Gold Bug Park, .9 of a mile from U.S. 50.

Several buildings on Georgetown's Main Street are typical Gold Rush structures—fire-resistant, single-story brick buildings with covered sidewalks and heavy iron doors.

The Jackson Area

Jackson-area mining camps have unexpected variety. Volcano and Fiddletown sit miles off Highway 49 in relative but delightful obscurity, especially compared to Jackson, which bustles with activity. Amador City is bisected by Highway 49, but it has considerable charm nonetheless. Many tourists miss Mokelumne Hill because it is off the main highway. Finally, Campo Seco is something very rare in the Mother Lode: a true ghost town.

Also in the area is the lovely community of Sutter Creek, which offers lots of trendy shops and upscale bed-and-breakfast establishments. A free, widely available walking tour will help you explore that town.

Jackson

With a population of almost 4,000, Jackson is not an appealing, rural community like most Gold Rush mining camps. For that reason, it would not be included in this book were it not for three attractions that the Highway 49 visitor simply must see.

In 1846, Jackson was a sleepy village called Bottileas (a misspelling of the Spanish word *botellas*) for the profusion of bottles left by travelers near a popular spring. In 1849, it was renamed for self-proclaimed "Colonel" Alden M. Jackson, a popular local lawyer, miner, merchant, and former Indian fighter. By the next year, when gold was found along Jackson Creek, the population grew to about 1,500. Jackson had more than mere placer deposits, and the hardrock mines, especially the Argonaut and Kennedy, kept Jackson prosperous despite an 1862 fire and an 1878 flood. Both mines were active until 1942, the year that Gold Limitation Order L-280 effectively closed mines not strategic to World War II. By the time they closed, the two mines had produced $60 million in gold.

Walking and Driving Around Jackson

Jackson's business district features several historic build-

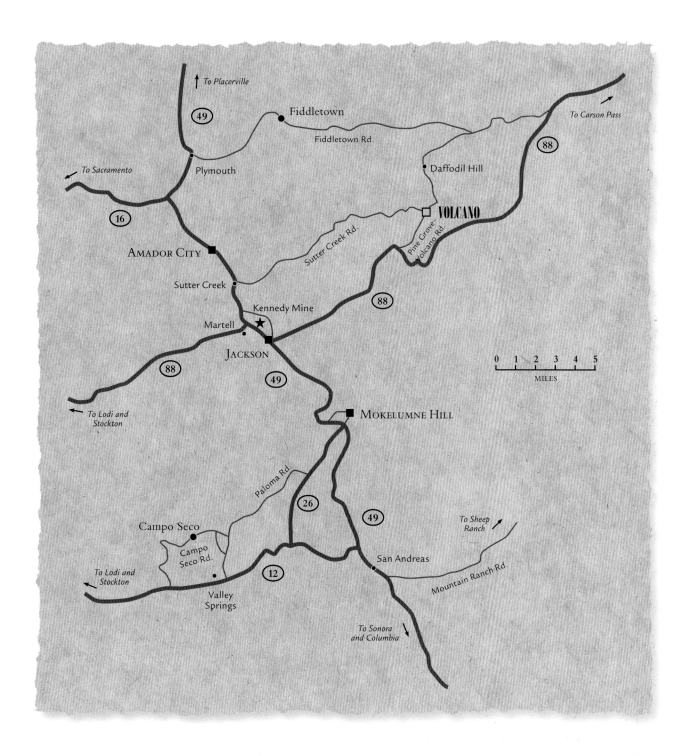

ings, including the National Hotel, an I.O.O.F. Hall, the Jackson Methodist Church, and St. Patrick's Catholic Church.

But the three aforementioned attractions that put Jackson in this book are all north of Jackson itself. The first, .4 of a mile north of downtown on North Main Street, is the 1894 St. Sava Church, the first Serbian Orthodox Church in the United States and one the loveliest churches in Gold Rush Country. Among the head-

stones in the surrounding cemetery is a mass grave for eleven of the forty-seven victims of the Argonaut Mining Disaster of August 27, 1922.

On your way to St. Sava you will pass three other Jackson cemeteries, including the large Catholic Cemetery, which also has a mass grave for victims of the Argonaut disaster.

The next attraction in Jackson is .6 of a mile north of St. Sava. There, housed in their own park, are the

Jackson's St. Sava Church has a delicate arch over the main gate and headstones surrounding the church.

enormous Kennedy Tailings Wheels. In 1912, the California state legislature passed an act requiring mines to impound their tailings, which had been polluting many of the state's streams and rivers, or cease operations within two years. This had an immediate effect upon the Argonaut and Kennedy mines. The Argonaut was able to comply easily, as an impound dam was built in a valley below the mine.

The Kennedy Mine was not as fortunate, because its only dam area was two hills away. To get the tailings to an impound dam, the Kennedy had to construct a series of lifts and flumes. The key to the operation was the four Kennedy Tailings Wheels. From an informational kiosk at the park, wheels numbers one and two are across the road to the north, and three and four are up a hill to the south.

The wheels lifted approximately 850 tons of tailings

every twenty-four hours to the impound dam. The tailings moved downhill by gravity to wheel number one. The wheel, with its 208 buckets, raised the tailings forty-two feet and dropped them into a flume to wheel number two, which again raised the tailings and sent them in a long flume across the valley, the valley in which the kiosk is located, to wheel number three. The lifting process repeated twice more, after which gravity took over and sent the tailings to the dam.

The Kennedy Tailings Wheels remain an impressive sight today. Numbers one and four are still standing, while two and three are down. If you want to see how the process worked, go to wheels one and two. You can see from wheel number one's flume how it passed the tailings to number two.

If you wish to walk a shorter distance, follow the path from the kiosk to wheel number four, where you can

Tailings Wheel Number Four stands as a reminder of the remarkable efforts that Jackson's Kennedy Mine went through to move tailings across a valley to a impound dam.

also see the impound dam in the distance.

Jackson's third outstanding attraction is the Kennedy Mine itself (see page 28).

When You Go
Jackson is 36 miles south of Placerville on Highway 49.

Volcano

Volcano is one of my favorite Mother Lode mining camps. Because it is a dozen miles off Highway 49, it has relatively few visitors. It has eschewed touristy touches and remains a peaceful, lovely town with friendly citizens and many excellent buildings.

In 1848, gold was discovered by discharged New York volunteers of the Mexican-American War. They called their young mining camp Volcano because they believed, erroneously, that the crater-like cup in which the town stood was volcanic. The soldiers-turned-miners even called the area's light gray-, yellow-, and reddish-colored stone "lava."

Where there was no lava, there certainly was gold. Working the placers of Soldier's Gulch, one miner netted $8,000 in a few days. Another extracted twenty-eight pounds of gold from a single pocket.

Volcano became a booming town of 5,000 citizens and could boast of such refinements as a thespian society, a debating society, a Miners' Library Association, a private law school, and an astronomical observatory, reportedly all "firsts" in California.

When placer deposits were exhausted in 1855, hydraulicking was used to uncover more gold, but the boom was over by 1865.

Walking and Driving Around Volcano
As you enter Volcano from the southwest, you will immediately face the town's most splendid building, the

The Kennedy Mine Tour

The Kennedy was the richest mine in this part of the Mother Lode and at one time was the deepest in the world, with a vertical shaft of 5,912 feet. It produced $35 million in gold before closing in 1942 after almost seventy-five years of operation.

The Kennedy Mine Tour is a surface tour; you do not go into the mine itself. And you would not want to, since the mine is a constant eighty-six degrees with 100 percent humidity. What the tour offers is an examination of more than a dozen above-ground structures.

The guided tour lasts slightly more than one-and-a-half hours, enjoyable for adults but too long, I believe, for many children. You may, however, purchase a brochure that allows you to follow the tour at your own pace and, perhaps, eliminate some areas. The stamp mill, for example, is roofless and very incomplete, and you could save about twenty minutes by bypassing it.

The Kennedy Mine's headframe is the largest still standing in the Mother Lode.

If you have the time, however, I highly recommend the informative and reasonably priced guided tour. The highlight comes at the three-story, 1907 mine office. You see retort and assay rooms as well as the payroll room with its imposing vault and safe—miners were paid in cash, with armed guards standing by.

At the end of the tour, you watch a short film made at the mine somewhere between 1914 and 1928. It is a perfect conclusion to your tour, because you will see the mine in full operation. Empty, gutted buildings like the stamp mill spring to life.

To reach the Kennedy Mine, take Highway 49 north from downtown Jackson for just over a mile, where a sign directs you to a right turn. At this writing, tours are given only on Saturday and Sunday between mid-March and October.

A hint of fall colors graces the limestone facade of the Kelly and Symonds Emporium, now the entrance to the Volcano Amphitheater.

Volcano's St. George Hotel, a three-story brick structure with wooden porches, was built somewhere between 1862 and 1867.

St. George Hotel.

Opposite the hotel is a small stone building and two large brick and limestone facades, the remains of the Clute Building and the Kelly and Symonds Emporium, two commercial structures that were joined together in 1861. Behind them lies Soldier's Gulch, the site of the original placer mining. Across the street stands the General Store, in continuous use since 1852.

East of the St. George, on the northwest corner of National and Plug streets, stands Volcano's schoolhouse, in use from 1855 until 1956 and now a private residence.

North on Plug Street at Emigrant Road is St. Bernard's Catholic Church, which dates from 1854 (although it was rebuilt in 1931). On a hill northeast of the church are the town's cemeteries.

Retrace your route on Plug Street and turn west on Consolation Street to see the wooden, two-story 1880 Union Hotel, now a private residence, which once went by the weighty title of the Union Hotel Billiards, Saloon, and Boarding House.

Beyond the hotel is the 1912 Armory Hall, followed by Old Abe, a bronze cannon cast in 1837 that was smuggled into Volcano in a hearse in 1862 by Union sympathizers, as a plaque succinctly puts it, to "discourage the rebel element." During the Civil War, Volcano gold went to support the Union cause. Old Abe never fired a shot, which was just as well, since the Unionists reportedly had no cannon balls, only river rocks.

Next door to Old Abe is the Sing Kee Store, built in 1854 or 1855 as both a general merchandise store and the Adams Express Agency office, the predecessor of Wells Fargo.

Attached to the back of the Sing Kee Store, but facing west, is the 1854 Masonic Lodge. It originally housed the Volcano *Weekly Ledger*, with office upstairs and press downstairs. By 1860 the building was used by both the Masons and the Odd Fellows.

Directly across the street from the Masonic Lodge is the 1871 jail. It looks rather insubstantial, with its outer walls of two-by-twelve timbers. Another identical wall is on the inside, but between the two is a layer of boiler plate. The incommodious jail features two small windows made of iron plate with small holes drilled in them.

When You Go

From Jackson, head northeast on State Route 88 to Pine Grove, a distance of 8.8 miles. Turn left on the Pine Grove–Volcano Road and follow it for 3.2 miles to Volcano.

Fiddletown

Missourians joining the Gold Rush settled this camp in 1849. Several stories account for the colorful place name.

One of them states that the settlers had brought their fiddles with them, and it was not uncommon to see one man working a claim while his partner played. Another tale claims that the town's name came not from musical fiddling at all: A town elder disparaged the younger good-for-nothings of the town by complaining that they were "always fiddling," especially when waiting for the rainy season to end.

After the placer deposits the Missourians found were depleted, both quartz mining and hydraulicking were moderately successful, but Fiddletown survived primarily as a trading center for nearby mines, which produced into the 1930s and 1940s, some utilizing dredges.

Walking and Driving Around Fiddletown

Fiddletown today is a delightfully unspoiled, rural place. If you are coming from Volcano, you will enter the community where Fiddletown Road meets American Flat Road. On the southwest corner is a Victorian home with nicely jigged gingerbread on its porch and eaves.

Across the street is the most imposing structure in town, the 1870 Schallhorn Building, a large, two-story structure, built of rhyolite tuff.

South from that intersection stands Fiddletown's schoolhouse and, across the street, the Fiddletown Cemetery, where there is a headstone touchingly expressing a widow's grief. It is for James Todd, who died in 1864, before his thirty-seventh birthday:

Oh Dear James,
I wait in hope on the promise given
We will meet up there in our home in heaven.
We met upon this lonely shore,
When shall we meet to part no more?

You passed a second, smaller cemetery on the way in from Volcano. To visit the I.O.O.F. Cemetery, take Fiddletown Road east for a half mile and turn left on a dirt road better suited for trucks. There you will find a cemetery of more than fifty graves. Unfortunately, there is also considerable evidence of vandalism.

Fiddletown's hub of activity for generations has been its quaint 1853 general store. At this writing the store is for sale and its hours are uncertain. I hope when you visit that it will once again be full of life. When I was there in the 1980s and early 1990s, a pot-bellied stove stood in the middle of the store, with nearby musical instruments begging for a session.

Beyond the general store is a community center with an oversized fiddle on its roof, a few brick and stone commercial buildings, and the wonderful Chew Kee Store—Fiddletown's most outstanding attraction.

Fiddletown's Schallhorn Building has served as a blacksmith and wagon shop, the overland mail's delivery site, and the express telegraph office.

The Chew Kee Store served Fiddletown's Chinese community with herbal remedies beginning in the 1850s.

Amador City is bisected by Highway 49 and has both brick and clapboard buildings on either side. At the bend in the road stands the elegant 1879 Imperial Hotel.

Built of rammed adobe earth with walls 2.5 feet thick, the Chew Kee Store was an herb shop operated by a Chinese doctor, Yee Fong Cheung, to provide traditional herbal remedies for Chinese miners. The store, now a museum, is fascinating because from the 1880s until 1965 it had but two owners, the first a Chinese known solely by the store's name of Chew Kee, and later by his adopted son, known as Jimmy Chow. Jimmy Chow kept the store as he had inherited it in 1913, so its herb drawers and shelves still hold the same remedies they did more than a century ago. At this writing it is open on Saturdays noon to 4 P.M. from April to October or by appointment.

When You Go
From Volcano, go east of town on Consolation Road, which becomes Rams Horn Grade. Rams Horn Grade dovetails into Shake Ridge Road in Daffodil Hill. Fiddletown Road heads west 6 miles from Volcano. Fiddletown is 10 miles ahead.

Amador City
Amador City could pose for a photo of what visitors expect a Gold Rush mining camp to look like. It has attractive, photogenic buildings and also contains, almost hidden from view, two interesting and photogenic cemeteries.

Rancher José Maria Amador and several Indians camped in this area in 1848 and began placer mining. In the fall of that year the first cabin was built by James Wheeler, a member of a gold-seeking party from Oregon. Within a year, a tent camp was spread out along Amador Creek.

The placer deposits had given out by 1851, but in that year four preachers found primary deposits at the Ministers' Claim, beginning the real prosperity of Amador City. Before quartz mining shut down in 1942, Amador City mines produced at least $34 million in gold.

When you enter Amador City from the north, the business section begins at a sharp bend of the highway. On the left stands the Imperial Hotel. Originally a general merchandise store, this two-story brick building later became a hotel and served in that capacity until 1927. When I first saw the Imperial, it was closed and shuttered, but it was completely restored in 1988 and serves as a hotel, restaurant, and bar.

The largest building on the east side of Highway 49 is the 1856 Amador Hotel. Beyond the hotel is a brick commercial building followed by a stone building that houses the Amador Whitney Museum.

On the west side of the highway are five false-front commercial buildings, including the 1870s-era Chichizola General Store and the Fleehart Building.

South of the business district is the 1881 Mine House, the former Keystone Mine headquarters that is now a bed and breakfast. Across the street is the looming headframe of the Keystone, from which was extracted $24.5 million in gold, accounting for about two-thirds of Amador City's total production.

To visit Amador City's two picturesque cemeteries, head east on Water Street, the road extending east from the Imperial Hotel. Pass the post office and turn left on East School Street. Climb the hill past the library (the former schoolhouse) and turn right on Bunker Hill Road. Only .1 of a mile later, turn left when Fremont Mine Road branches to the right. As you descend into a valley, you will be able to see the Oak Knoll Cemetery below. In .3 of a mile there is a gate on the road's west side, beyond the house at 14501 Bunker Hill Road, that leads you to the cemetery.

The peaceful Oak Knoll Cemetery was established in 1905, but graves predate its official standing. A wonderful verse graces the stone of Johanna Pryor, who died at age thirty-seven in 1882: "Amiable, she won all. Intelligent, she charmed all. Fervent, she loved all. And dead, she saddened all."

To visit the other cemetery, return the way you came, but before you reach the library on East School Street, turn right on Church Street, which will curve around to the south. As you pass O'Neill Street, you will see the Amador City Cemetery, in use between 1851 and 1892, on your left.

When You Go

From Fiddletown, drive 5.8 miles west on Fiddletown Road to Plymouth and Highway 49. Take 49 south for 6 miles to Amador City.

Mokelumne Hill

In 1817, Father Narcisco Duran, writing in his diary of his exploits on the Sacramento and San Joaquin rivers, mentioned an Indian tribe called the Muquelemnes. The name, which evolved to Mokelumne ("moe-*kull*-uh-mee"), was later given to a river you will cross coming south from Jackson on Highway 49. Miners from Oregon worked that river in 1848. A rise south of the river, where a trading post stood, was known as Mokelumne Hill.

The Gold Rush town took the name of the hill, but miners called it "Mok (pronounced "moke") Hill" for short.

Americans, French, Chileans, and Chinese all lived in the booming town, but the Americans, claiming property rights, eventually took over the Chilean and French claims. They apparently coexisted with the Chinese without such confrontations, as Mok Hill had a sizable Chinatown.

The community was a particularly violent place and once recorded at least one murder per week for seventeen weeks. Part of the reason for the violence might have been the simple press of humanity: The demand for mining rights was so strong that claims were restricted to a mere sixteen feet square. Miners were practically panning or digging on top of each other.

There was plenty to pursue, however. Four Frenchmen retrieved 138 pounds of gold in a single gulch. Another miner found an eighty-ounce piece of pure gold shaped like a pot hook.

As the placers gave out, quartz mining and then hydraulic mining took over, but people began to exit the town in the early 1860s. Mokelumne Hill lost the Calaveras County seat in 1866.

Walking and Driving Around Mokelumne Hill

Before you enter Mokelumne Hill on historic route 49, you will pass the large Protestant Cemetery, which features a loop road. One epitaph is for William Beals, who died at age thirty-four: "His death was caused by burns received at the destruction of the Poland Hotel, San Joaquin County, on the 8th of July 1859."

Adjacent to the Protestant Cemetery is the Pioneer Jewish Cemetery, with stones dating from 1859. The markers, for natives of Germany and Prussia, are, with one exception, in both Hebrew and English.

Mokelumne Hill is .1 of a mile beyond those cemeteries. The first buildings you will see are the roofless 1854 L. Mayer & Son Store on your left and the 1855 Wells Fargo Office, originally Levinson's Store, on your right.

A rusting but restorable Dodge truck, complete with a 1956 license plate, stands next to the stone ruins of Mokelumne Hill's L. Mayer & Son Store.

Next to the Mayer building, where Center and Main streets meet, is the 1854 I.O.O.F. Hall. East of that hall is an 1854 stone and frame commercial building known as the Italian Store. By 1889 it was owned by Chung Kee and bordered Chinatown, which is located in China Gulch, immediately beyond the store.

If you continue east on Center past Main through China Gulch, you will arrive at the St. Thomas Aquinas Catholic Cemetery. This graveyard also has a loop drive. Many of the stones are for natives of Ireland, France, and Italy.

Now return to Center and Main. The business district features several more historic buildings, including one of Mok Hill's loveliest structures, built in 1851 of brick and rhyolite tuff as the Hotel de France and rebuilt after an 1874 fire. It is now known as the Hotel Leger.

Down the block is the 1856 Mokelumne Hill Community Church, originally California's first Congregational Church.

To see the 1864 community school, now a private residence, turn east on Church Street from Main. Go two blocks and turn north on Old School Way. The large wooden former school is easy to pick out because of its belfry.

Continue on Old School Way and turn east on Lafayette Street. On the corner of Lafayette and Marlette streets stands the St. Thomas Aquinas Catholic Church.

When You Go

From Jackson, drive 6.4 miles south on Highway 49. That highway bypasses Mokelumne Hill, but "historic" State

34

The I.O.O.F. Hall at "Mok Hill" was originally the two-story Adams Express Agency office. Made of rhyolite tuff carved into blocks, the structure became the first three-story building in the Mother Lode when the Odd Fellows added a story in 1861.

Route 49 leaves modern Highway 49 with a left turn at that point. That route leads to Mokelumne Hill in .9 of a mile.

Campo Seco

Campo Seco (Spanish for "dry camp") was settled in 1849 by Mexicans. "Seco" was the operant word: A thriving town in 1850, it had lost half its population by the end of that year because scarce water sent prospectors elsewhere. In 1853, however, two Mexicans who stayed extracted $5,700 in gold in one morning in Sullivans Gulch.

Although the town was settled because of placer gold, it was the copper and zinc deposits at the Penn Mine, which opened in the 1860s and lasted until the 1940s, that provided the greatest prosperity.

That same mine is the site of an enormous environmental cleanup at this writing. In addition, some of the area is off limits because it is the habitat of the endangered Valley Elderberry Longhorn Beetle. As I looked at the protective fencing and stern warnings about the beetle, I considered how early-day miners, who ran roughshod over the land, would react to being excluded from a potential gold site by a bug.

The Adams Express Agency Building, on the east side of Campo Seco Road, provides the town's most photogenic remnants. West of those ruins on Penn Mine Road are two mortared stone ruins that were part of the Chinese community. Surrounding them are *ailanthus altissima*, the "Tree-of-Heaven" that Chinese often brought from their native land.

Above: *Almost all of the decorative plaster has eroded from the mortared stone remnants of Campo Seco's Adams Express Agency Building.*

Right: *Campo Seco's one-room schoolhouse stands along College Street. One wonders if the town's founding fathers named the street to inspire their youth.*

Facing page: *An unusual rock lintel in a kind of keystone pattern graces this stone ruin in the Chinese section of Campo Seco.*

South of the Adams Express building is A. Pereira's General Store, shuttered at this writing, which served the community for decades. South of the store are remnants of another stone building.

Farther south of town on the east side of the road stands an attractive Victorian home with an offset triple-bay window. Across the street, heading west, is College Street, which leads to Campo Seco's old schoolhouse.

Adjacent to the school is the Protestant Cemetery, where there are more than fifty graves. One poignant epitaph is for Elizabeth Kester, who died in 1878 at thirty-eight years: "She sleeps in the grave with her baby."

South on Campo Seco Road .2 of a mile from College Street is the Catholic Cemetery, where natives of Spain (including members of the Pereira family), Ireland, France, and Chile are buried.

When You Go

Campo Seco is 11 miles southwest of Mokelumne Hill. From Main Street, drive south to Highway 49. Turn left and then take an immediate right onto State Route 26, the road to Valley Springs. In 3.6 miles, turn right on Paloma Road. In 5.5 miles, you will come to Campo Seco Road. Turn right. In another mile turn right again, which actually keeps you on Campo Seco Road, and proceed one mile to the townsite.

Columbia's Wells Fargo Office, built in 1858 by William Daegner, was in service until 1917.

The Columbia Area

During the Gold Rush, the town of Columbia was hailed as the "Gem of the Southern Mines." A hundred and fifty years later, the "gem" remains unflawed. Columbia, now a state park, features attractions such as restaurants, shops, stagecoach rides, a hotel, a theater, and even a saloon. But despite all this activity, Columbia retains a dignity that makes it a most enjoyable place.

The other mining camps in the Columbia area include Murphys, one of the most picturesque towns in the Mother Lode; Sheep Ranch, a somnolent site with a few attractive buildings and one very handsome one; Chinese Camp, which features a photogenic, deserted main street; and Knights Ferry, which showcases one of the three covered bridges in this book.

Other more-bustling towns worth exploring, but not incorporated in this book, include Sonora, Jamestown, and Angels Camp.

Columbia

The Mother Lode consisted of one incredible place to find gold after another, but fortuitous Columbia is geo-

logically unique: It sits on a limestone bed pockmarked with potholes that for thousands of years conveniently collected placer gold, seemingly waiting for someone to retrieve it.

That someone was Dr. Thaddeus Hildreth in 1850, who camped in the area with a group of prospectors. The gold was so plentiful that others swarmed to the new camp, first called Hildreth's Diggings, later American Camp, and finally Columbia.

Despite an acute shortage of water (eventually solved with an elaborate series of flumes and ditches), Columbia prospered wildly, becoming a town of 6,000—the biggest camp in the Mother Lode. Although Columbia now has the permanence of brick, it began, like other mining camps, as a mere tent city, with an occasional rough-sawn wood structure. After fires in 1854 and 1857, it was rebuilt with locally made brick and fireproof iron doors shipped from eastern states.

As placer gold gave out in the 1860s, Columbia declined. By the 1880s its population had dropped to about 500, but not before an estimated $87 million in gold

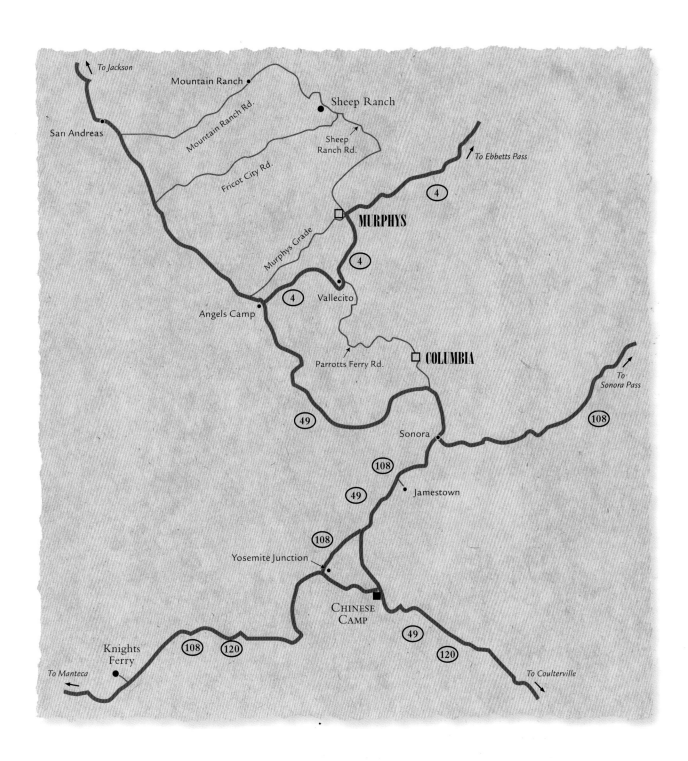

To Jackson

Mountain Ranch

Sheep Ranch

Mountain Ranch Rd.

San Andreas

Sheep Ranch Rd.

To Ebbetts Pass

Fricot City Rd.

(4)

MURPHYS

Murphys Grade

(4)

(4) Vallecito

Angels Camp

Parrotts Ferry Rd.

COLUMBIA

To Sonora Pass

(49)

Sonora

(108)

(108)

(49)

Jamestown

(108)

Yosemite Junction

CHINESE CAMP

(49)

Knights Ferry

(108) (120)

(120)

To Manteca

To Coulterville

The drug store in Columbia was operated by doctors G. A. Field and J. McChesney. After the original burned in 1854, this structure was built in 1856.

had been shipped from "The Gem of the Southern Mines."

Walking Around Columbia

Columbia retains its Gold Rush atmosphere better than any other sizable Mother Lode town. One reason is that automobiles are not allowed within its interior streets. Another is that shops selling wares are not permitted to display gaudy, touristy signs.

A third reason Columbia is so delightful is that it is a living history museum (with no admission fee) where salespeople dress in period attire, a strolling folk singer plays traditional instruments while singing nineteenth-century songs, and a blacksmith uses hundred-year-old tools to create his wares. You can ride in an authentic stagecoach, watch a play, or stay the night in a 150-year-old hotel.

Columbia has too many attractions to list them all, but I found the most enjoyment in buildings in which there was little or nothing for sale, such as the 1858 Wells Fargo Express Building, on the south end of Main Street, which has a chalkboard announcing the stages "arriving" and "departing" as well as freight ready to be "shipped."

You need to explore Columbia carefully to see more than the obvious attractions. For example, hidden behind the Wells Fargo Building is a well-equipped assay office that would be easy to overlook.

The two largest "ghost town" state parks in California are Columbia and Bodie (see chapter five). The principal difference between them is exemplified in Columbia's Franco cabin at the southwest corner of Main and Jackson streets. When you look through this cabin's windows, you see a home ready for a drill sergeant's inspection: Clothes are hung on hooks; dishes are neatly stacked; the bed is made. On a small table is an unfinished "letter": "My Dear Wife, I take pen in hand to tell you about my fortunes in the . . ." One almost expects Mr. Franco to appear through a doorway.

Bodie is vastly different. The same cabin there would

This pharmacist's journal describes how to prepare, among other remedies, "Compound Amica Liniment."

have items left scattered about in abandonment: a bed with no mattress, a child's broken toy, and dust everywhere. No one can mistake a Bodie cabin for one that has life.

Personally, I am very glad the two state parks are so different, as each has a distinct feel for history. It is wonderful not to have to choose between the two.

An often-overlooked building is the 1860 Columbia School. An enjoyable way to reach it is on foot, taking the "Old School Trail" from Pacific and Columbia streets. The attractive two-story brick building last saw students in 1937, when it was deemed unsafe during an earthquake.

Behind the schoolhouse are three of Columbia's four cemeteries, the public cemetery (with "In God We Trust" on a wooden arch over the entrance) and adjacent graveyards for the Masons and Odd Fellows. (The fourth cemetery, the Catholic, stands next to St. Anne's Church on Kennebec Hill, south of town.)

In the public cemetery stand an interesting matching pair of headstones. The first is for Joel A. Cumback, who died in 1857 at age thirty. The stone was erected by his friend, Jacob R. Giddis. Next to Cumback's grave lies that friend, who was murdered four years later at age twenty-eight.

When You Go

From downtown Sonora, take Highway 49 north for 2.3 miles to Parrotts Ferry Road. Follow it for 1.7 miles to Columbia Historic State Park.

Murphys

Murphys is another of my favorite Gold Rush mining camps. Its central business district, with its streets lined with locust trees, invites a stroll. In fact, staying the night and walking Murphys' streets in the evening is a requirement for each of my Mother Lode visits.

Murphys is named for John M. Murphy, who came to California from Canada in 1844. Four years later, John

Above: *The Columbia Schoolhouse has an outside rear staircase to reach the second-story classroom and, nearby, a two-door, six-hole outhouse (on right).*

Facing page, top: *A thirty-one-star flag (California entered the Union in 1850 as the thirty-first state) hangs above the 1855 justice court, which is active today.*

Facing page, bottom: *An exhibit of a Chinese herb shop and temple stands in an 1860s building that actually served Columbia's citizens as a bakery.*

and his brother Daniel camped along Angels Creek at a place later known as Murphys New Diggings but shortened to Murphys when it received a post office in 1851. By that time, the Murphy brothers were long gone. They opened a trading post to sell to the hordes of hopeful miners, made their fortune, and left town in 1849.

Early claims were restricted to a tiny eight feet square; nevertheless, one claim is said to have yielded thirty-seven pounds of gold one afternoon and another sixty-three pounds the following morning.

Murphys' peak year was 1855, but, like dozens of other camps, the town began declining in the 1860s despite attempts at hardrock and hydraulic mining.

Walking and Driving Around Murphys

Main Street features a number of excellent buildings, with the most obvious the rough-quarried limestone Murphys Hotel, at the southwest corner of Main and Algiers streets. It opened in 1856 as the Sperry and Perry Hotel and was later known as Mitchler's Hotel. It became the Murphys Hotel in 1945.

The Murphys Hotel has a register containing the names of some of America's most famous figures: Mark Twain, Horatio Alger Jr., J. Pierpont Morgan, and Ulysses S. Grant. It also features one of California's most infamous: Charles E. Bolton, the highwayman Black Bart.

Diagonally across from the hotel is the former Jones' Apothecary Shop. Constructed after an 1859 fire, it was built never to burn: In addition to its limestone and brick walls and its iron doors, it has no windows in the three walls not facing the street. It later became the I.O.O.F. Hall and in 1886 became Ben and James Stephens' store. An old painted sign on the building's west side announces that business: "Stephens Bro's. Cheap Cash Store."

West on Main and across from a modern section of the Murphys Hotel is the 1856 Peter L. Traver Building, which features a Gold Rush-era museum open Friday through Sunday. Attached to the Traver Building on the west is the Thompson Building, built around 1856. On its western exterior wall is the amusing and anecdotal Wall of Comparative Ovations, which commemorates pioneers and honorable members of E Clampus Vitus, a mock-serious benevolent brotherhood that erects historical plaques throughout the West. The organization, a burlesque (beginning with its pseudo-Latin name) of secret fraternal orders, began in California during the Gold Rush and was revived in the 1930s.

The Murphys Hotel features both old and modern buildings. In the original portion, rebuilt in 1860 after an 1856 fire, the rooms are authentically furnished.

A plaque on St. Patrick's Catholic Church states that the church was originally located near Jones' Apothecary Shop. That building was destroyed by fire, but according to an historical plaque, "the chalice and other sacred appurtenances were carried to safety by 'Auntie' Moran in her voluminous apron."

The former Murphys Grammar School, built in 1860, was continuously in use until 1973. It was called "Pine Grove College" by its pupils, one of whom, physicist Albert Michelson, was the first American to win a Nobel prize.

St. Patrick's Catholic Church is located .2 of a mile north of the business district at 619 Sheep Ranch Road. The attractive church was begun in 1858 and dedicated in 1861. A well-kept cemetery is within the church grounds.

To visit another cemetery, head east from downtown Murphys on Main. Jones Street veers off to the right behind a large monument. Follow Jones for .2 of a mile to the turnoff to the Buena Vista Cemetery, which has hundreds of graves in a pleasant, tree-lined and flower-filled setting.

Immediately east of the cemetery entrance is the former Murphys Grammar School.

When You Go

From Columbia, proceed north on Parrotts Ferry Road for 9.8 miles. Turn right on State Route 4 and go 3.3 miles. Turn left on Main Street and follow it .4 of a mile to enter downtown Murphys.

Sheep Ranch

My three visits to Sheep Ranch have all been during lazy afternoons. Perhaps it is Sheep Ranch itself that causes such indolence. On one visit I was there for over an hour and saw not another human, not even a car passing through. The only activity, and that was slight enough, was from—appropriately—a small herd of sheep grazing next door to the empty general store.

The town was once very different. The Sheep Ranch Mine was located in 1866 and named for a nearby sheep corral. In 1874, George Hearst (the father of famous newspaper magnate William Randolph Hearst) and some associates acquired the mine, beginning Hearst's fortune. Hearst sold the mine in 1893, by which time it had yielded about $4 million in gold. It was reactivated in 1899 and worked intermittently until 1942, producing another $3 million.

Walking and Driving Around Sheep Ranch

When you enter Sheep Ranch, the most obvious landmark is the modern volunteer fire department, located at a bend in Sheep Ranch Road. The central part of town is directly west of the fire department on Main Street.

On your right as you proceed down Main is a small, stout brick structure that likely was a vault or powderhouse. Beyond it is the shuttered board-and-batten general store and post office. Nearby are several wooden residences, most vacant.

Farther west on Main is the town's principal attraction, the Pioneer Hotel, now a private residence. The Pioneer has an unusual history. It was brought as a one-story building from the vicinity of Mountain Ranch to this location in about 1868. In 1899, the building was jacked up and a first story constructed underneath it, a creative way of adding a second story to a building that already has a roof. The hotel's attractive surrounding porches were added at the same time.

Another building of note is the small, red 1911 schoolhouse, now privately owned, standing on a low hill behind the fire department.

If you wish to visit the town cemetery, return to Sheep Ranch Road and head back toward Murphys. Armstrong Road almost immediately heads obliquely to the left. Take Armstrong for .3 of a mile to the graveyard, where you will find about three dozen graves. As you near the cemetery, you pass a wooden structure on your right that once served as a store.

When You Go

From Murphys, take Sheep Ranch Road, which begins one block west of Algiers on Main Street, for 8.5 miles to Sheep Ranch. At 6.2 miles from Murphys there is a junction; take the left to stay on Sheep Ranch Road.

Above: *A boarded-up general store and post office (left) and what likely was a vault or powderhouse (far right) stand in somnolent Sheep Ranch.*

Left: *Sheep Ranch's 1911 schoolhouse was built in part from lumber from a previous school. Students last attended classes there in 1955.*

Above: *The doctor's home, office, and board-inghouse is the only building made com-pletely of wood on Chinese Camp's Main Street.*

Right: *The Buck Store in Chinese Camp is unusual in that it is a brick and stone building but has a wooden false front.*

Chinese Camp's St. Francis Xavier Church, built in 1855, also has a cemetery with about a dozen old graves, most for natives of Ireland.

Chinese Camp

Because Chinese Camp is the last unrestored Mother Lode mining camp (at least at this writing), it is well worth a visit. Its Main Street absolutely invites a sketch pad.

The Chinese were the people most discriminated against during the Gold Rush, although all minorities received their unfair share. Americans felt they essentially had a proprietary right to the best claims. Therefore, when a place of relative tolerance could be found, Chinese flocked to that haven.

Most Chinese had no intention of settling permanently in America. They were primarily young single or married men hoping to make great sums from the Gold Rush, send the money home to their families, and eventually return. If a man was married, for example, his wife would customarily stay in China with his parents.

Chinese Camp was the oldest town populated by Chinese, settled in 1849 at a place first known as Washington Camp. Later known as Chinese Diggings and then Chinese (or even Chinee) Camp, it received its post office in 1854. By that time, it had a population of 5,000, as many as half of them non-Asian.

Although the Chinese were targets of discrimination, that did not mean they were always a united people. Secret societies called tongs, based upon one's home area in China, were prevalent where there were large numbers of Chinese.

Two of those tongs had a violent skirmish near Chinese Camp in 1856, apparently caused by a large rock rolling from one group's diggings into the other's. The subsequent Tong War, as it came to be known, involved over 2,000 men wielding daggers, axes, spears, and even a

few muskets. Four men died during the resulting mayhem, and 250 were jailed afterward.

Placer mining, which lasted into the 1870s, yielded an estimated $2.5 million in gold. The town also served as an important transportation hub.

Walking Around Chinese Camp

Chinese Camp today consists of almost a dozen buildings in various states of decay among a proliferation of ailanthus trees, the traditional Chinese "Tree-of-Heaven."

The Chinese Camp Store stands prominently near the intersection of Highway 49 and State Route 120. Go south from the store to a historical monument and park there, as the town's Main Street is around the corner.

The first commercial building on the north side of the street is the 1854 Timothy McAdams Store, which served as both a general store and the post office. Its postal boxes were accessible from the outside.

Next door to the McAdams Store is a two-story wooden residence that was a doctor's home, office, and boardinghouse. Across the street is one standing wall of the 1849 office of the Adams Express Agency, later Wells Fargo. Its iron doors now reside in the Wells Fargo Museum in San Francisco. West of that wall was a building, now gone, that was a combination livery stable and brewery. (One wonders if they had the area's happiest horses or the worst-tasting beer.)

Next door to the doctor's house is a brick building with iron doors that was a foundry and blacksmith shop. John Studebaker, who later made wheelbarrows for miners in Coloma and Placerville before becoming an Indiana automobile builder, learned his trade in that shop, according to a town resident.

Across the street from the foundry is the Buck Store, a

brick and stone building with a wooden false front. Next door is a large, two-story, wood-frame structure on the corner of Main Street and Red Hills Road that was a fandango parlor and house of prostitution.

Across Highway 49 on Main Street is the attractive St. Francis Xavier Catholic Church and Cemetery. Visible from the church is the old school, now a private residence, with its fading red, pagoda-style roof.

A tiny city cemetery, with six headstones, is located west of the school and just east of the highway. Although Chinese were the town's principal residents, one would not expect to find graves of Chinese there: It was traditional to return their remains to their native land. For an elaboration on that tradition, see the Weaverville entry (chapter three).

When You Go
Chinese Camp is 10 miles southwest of Sonora on Highway 49.

Knights Ferry

Although Knights Ferry is often overlooked in tours of the Mother Lode, the town was important as both a commerce center for the Gold Rush and, later, as a mining town in its own right. Today it is well worth visiting for its dozing downtown and its marvelous covered bridge.

Knights Ferry was founded by William Knight, a scout, fur trader, and pre–Gold Rush California pioneer. Beginning in 1848, he operated a ferry across the Stanislaus River on a route connecting the Mother Lode to Stockton, an important supply point. When he died in 1849 in a gunfight, the ferry was taken over by John and Lewis Dent. The brothers, whose sister was married to Ulysses S. Grant, also built a flour mill and a sawmill. In 1852, ferry service over the Stanislaus ended with the construction of a bridge, which was washed away in an 1862 flood. A replacement bridge, the one standing today, opened in 1863. At about the same time, placer deposits were discovered along the river, and Knights Ferry enjoyed a gold boom of its own.

Walking and Driving Around Knights Ferry
My recommendation is simple: town first, bridge last. On your right as you enter this small, quiet community is the wood-frame Knights Ferry Hotel, operating since 1854. Beyond the hotel, on the corner of Sonora and Dean streets, is The Store, in continuous service since 1852. It features a 1893 potbellied stove, an old safe, and a working antique telephone.

Across Dean Street from The Store is Miller's Saloon.

An attached plaque calls Fred Miller's place "the finest bar, pool hall, card room, and dance hall in the area."

West of Miller's stands the 1870 two-story I.O.O.F. Hall, which, like many fraternal halls in the Mother Lode, had a store on the first floor and the lodge upstairs.

On the corner of Sonora and Ellen streets stands the Masonic Lodge. Next door is an attractive two-story residence featuring a block facade.

To visit the Oak Grove Cemetery, take Sonora Road beyond Ellen and turn left onto Cemetery Road. Inside the graveyard, near a tin-covered water tower, you will find a "cradle grave," a small metal fence with an arch over it enclosing a grave. On the arch is a simple metal sign: "Our Baby."

When you return to town, turn left on Ellen Street in front of the Masonic Lodge and go to Shurl Street to see the 1860 Methodist Episcopal Church, rebuilt in 1900.

To see the covered bridge, the primary attraction of Knights Ferry, return through town to the Knights Ferry Recreation Area on Covered Bridge Road. A visitors' center features several exhibits on the area's history, along with specimens of native fauna.

Along the path to the bridge, you will pass a flour mill that was later converted to a hydroelectric power plant. Water rushing through a penstock caused a turbine to turn, producing power through a generator. The penstock, turbine, and generator are still visible in the building.

Beyond the power plant is the covered bridge, the first of three in this book, so perhaps it is worth mentioning why covered bridges exist at all. Wood that constantly gets wet and then dries will crack, weakening the bridge itself, so a structure was built over the bridge to protect it from the elements. It had nothing to do with the comfort of people crossing the bridge.

As mentioned earlier, the original bridge across the Stanislaus River lasted five years before a flood took it out. The second bridge, the one you see today, was built eight feet higher than the first and supported by three piers of local stone sharpened on the upstream side to deflect water.

When You Go
From Chinese Camp, take State Route 120 northwest for 3.5 miles to Yosemite Junction and turn left on State Routes 108 and 120. Go 13 miles to Sonora Road and turn right. Knights Ferry is less than a mile from that junction on Sonora Road.

The 330-foot long Knights Ferry Bridge, built in 1863, is the longest covered bridge west of the Mississippi River.

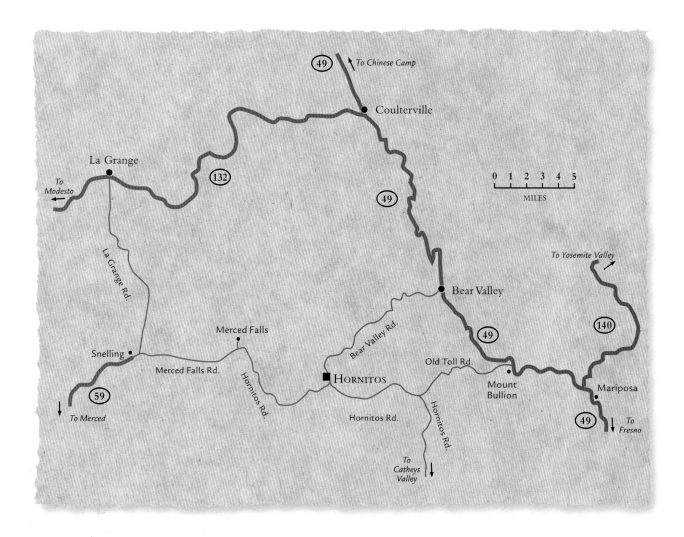

The Coulterville Area

The southernmost mining camps of the Mother Lode extend south from Coulterville. All are less visited than vibrant towns like Sonora and Jamestown. Included in this area are Coulterville, which offers several historic buildings and an attractive cemetery; Bear Valley, a minor site with a few vintage structures; Hornitos, a sleepy town that is a personal favorite of mine; and La Grange, which is often not included in Mother Lode tour books but which features several worthwhile attractions.

Coulterville

Pennsylvanian George W. Coulter opened a tent store in 1850 to supply hundreds of miners working nearby placer diggings. The first permanent building was erected by the Francisco Bruschi family. When the post office was established in 1853, it was for Maxwells Creek, in honor of Coulter's partner, miner George Maxwell. The town kept that name until 1872, when it was changed to Coulterville. At its peak, the town featured ten hotels and twenty-five saloons with a population of an estimated 3,000 Americans and about 1,000 Chinese.

Two of the Coulterville area's most productive mines were in the Malvina Group and the Mary Harrison Group. The former was active from the 1850s until 1942, producing more than $1 million in gold. The latter, active from 1852 until the early 1900s, yielded about $1.5 million in gold.

Walking and Driving Around Coulterville

The largest historic building in Coulterville today is the Hotel Jeffery, which stands at the center of town at the intersection of Highway 49 and Main Street. The Jeffery was built in 1850 or 1851 as a store with a dance hall on the second floor and converted to a hotel in 1852. A third story was added during one of the hotel's several renovations.

Mining machinery stands in front of the ruins of the Coulterville Hotel. Behind is the Hotel Jeffery, purchased by George Jeffery in 1870. It stayed in the same family for three generations.

A fading sign proclaims this Coulterville market as the "Chinatown Groc.," but it was much better known as the Sun Sun Wo Store.

Across Highway 49 west of the hotel is the 1856 Wells Fargo office and McCarthy's Store, with the painted reminder on the north wall that "Stanislaus IS the Best Flour." Attached to that store are the roofless ruins of the 1860 Coulterville Hotel and, behind the hotel, the Northern Mariposa County History Center.

Along Main Street heading northeast from Highway 49 are several historic buildings, including the 1880 Bruschi Bros. General Merchandise, and, farther up the street, the 1900 I.O.O.F. Hall.

If you continue northeast on Main you will come to Chinatown Main Street and the lone remaining building of the once-thriving Chinatown, the Sun Sun Wo Store. Built about 1851, it is one of only a few adobe structures left in the Mother Lode.

Between downtown Coulterville and the Sun Sun Wo Store is the Public Cemetery, located .2 of a mile north of Main Street on Cemetery Street. Among the graves are members of the Coulter and Jeffery families. One touching grave is a twin marker for sisters Emma and Mary Thompson, who were born three years apart but died on the same day—Emma's fifteenth birthday.

When You Go

Coulterville is 18.2 miles southeast of Chinese Camp along Highway 49.

Bear Valley

Here is a town that once suffered from an identity crisis. Between 1850 and 1858, the site was called Haydensville, Biddleville, Simpsonville, Johnsonville, and finally Bear Valley.

Placer gold was found in the camp of many names by Mexicans in 1850, who were pushed from their claims by Americans, but not before the Mexicans had taken out about $250,000 in gold.

At its peak, Bear Valley had an estimated 3,000 citizens. Placer gold gave out in 1852, but quartz mining continued into the turn of the twentieth century, with a stamp mill still operating in 1903.

In Bear Valley, pioneer explorer John C. Frémont had a 44,386-acre ranch, La Mariposas Estate, which served as the Frémont family home from 1858 until 1861. He sold the estate in 1863 for $6 million (in 1847 he had purchased it for $3,200). Frémont also owned at least two mines, the Pine Tree and the Josephine.

Bear Valley today is a minor site on the way to the more interesting town of Hornitos, but you should definitely stop to look.

The 1862 Simpson and Trabucco Store in Bear Valley was made of stone, but it had a faux covering to make it appear to be cut block.

On the north end of Bear Valley is Mrs. Trabucco's Store, built in 1880. Across Bear Valley Road stands the 1862 I.O.O.F. Hall—now a museum—and the 1862 Simpson and Trabucco Store, still open for business.

Beyond the Simpson and Trabucco Store is the roofless ruin of the Bon Ton Saloon, which has a faux stone block false front. Next door is the more modern Bon Ton Cafe.

The road to the schoolhouse and the Catholic and Bear Valley cemeteries is posted as "private."

When You Go

Bear Valley is 16 miles southeast of Coulterville on Highway 49.

Hornitos

Hornitos is one of the most picturesque mining camps in California, looking more like its nineteenth-century self than most towns of Gold Rush Country. On one of my visits, I was virtually alone, and, as I stood in the town's silent Mexican-style plaza, I almost felt myself projected back in time.

If I had been successful with that projection, I would not have seen a silent Mexican village but rather one of the rowdiest mining camps in California. A visitor in 1857 remarked that he felt "outside the pale of civilization."

Hornitos was established by Mexican miners who had been driven out of Quartzburg, two miles northeast of Hornitos, in 1852. The name is Spanish for "little ovens," and most books relate that the name comes either from small ovens erected there or from Mexican graves that looked like small ovens. Erwin G. Gudde, however, in his esteemed *California Place Names*, states that "the name is doubtless a transfer name, probably from *Los Hornitos*, in the Mexican state of Durango."

The town received its post office in 1856. By 1860, several thousand people lived in Hornitos, including many from Quartzburg, who joined the very people they had exiled. A stamp mill at the Jenny Lind Mine (named for P. T. Barnum's "Swedish Nightingale") was reported to have crushed $1,000 in gold daily. Another source claims that the town's Wells Fargo office was shipping $40,000 in gold per day to a private mint, operated in nearby Mount Ophir under authorization from the federal government.

Walking Around Hornitos

As you enter Hornitos from Bear Valley, on your right will be an adobe structure with iron doors. It is followed by a wooden barn and then Gagliardo and Company General Merchandise, which opened in 1854. Across the street is a stone structure attached to a larger brick commercial building sporting an old gas pump.

Bear Valley Road then veers to the right as High Street

The Gagliardo and Co. General Merchandise in Hornitos features some intricate brick work—note the inset areas with vertical bricks over the lintels.

goes left. Take the right to the old plaza and park. This is a town to explore on foot.

The post office sits on the western side of the tiny plaza. The postmistress told me that the building on the north side of the plaza was a saloon and dance hall. She also informed me that the local pronunciation of the town is not the Spanish "or-*neet*-ose" but rather "hor-*neet*-us."

On the south side of the plaza is a Gold Rush–era building that is a popular watering hole. Immediately south of that bar is a Masonic Lodge, which was built of native rock around 1855 and purchased by the Masons in 1873. It is the oldest and smallest single-story Masonic lodge in California.

Another historic building is the large ruin of the Ghirardelli Store, which is across the street and just north of the plaza. Domenico Ghirardelli's company, which has purveyed chocolate and cocoa since 1852, operated out of this structure beginning in 1859. The chocolate company still owns the property.

The street behind the Ghirardelli Store is High Street, which features the old jail, with its two-foot-thick granite walls.

From the jail, walk north to St. Catherine Street and climb the hill to St. Catherine's Catholic Church.

The adjoining cemetery has at least one native of

When you visit Hornitos, walk around the ruins of the Ghirardelli Store. It is a much larger building than it appears to be.

St. Catherine's Catholic Church is an attractive 1862 wooden structure with a stone foundation and buttresses added in the 1930s. It also has an even more modern feature not readily apparent— aluminum siding.

France, but most graves are for Italians. A second cemetery, the public one, is on a road with a locked gate beyond the town's landfill. One section of it appears to be for I.O.O.F. members.

Southeast of town .2 of a mile, on the road to Mt. Bullion, stands the 1860s Hornitos School.

When You Go

Hornitos is 10.1 miles southwest of Bear Valley on County Road J16, Bear Valley Road. Bear Valley Road intersects Highway 49 just south of Mrs. Trabucco's Store in Bear Valley.

La Grange

French Argonauts originally founded the community of French Bar along the Tuolumne River in 1849 or 1850. Floods in 1851 and 1852 encouraged them to relocate their camp above the flood plain to its present location. When the town received its post office in 1854, it took the name La Grange, probably in honor of Lafayette's country estate in France.

The town's population peaked at about 5,000. When placer deposits were depleted in 1859, La Grange prospered as an agricultural community, although quartz and hydraulic mining were pursued with limited success.

After the turn of the twentieth century, La Grange had a rebirth as a mining town when dredging of the Tuolumne River extracted $13 million in gold, ending in 1949. A local former dredge worker told me that operations ceased because the price of everything went up after World War II, but not the price of gold, making dredging unprofitable. He thinks plenty of gold remains in the sands of the Tuolumne.

Walking and Driving Around La Grange

As you enter La Grange from the west, on your right is the two-story, wood-frame 1880 I.O.O.F. Hall.

East of the hall stands the best building in town, the 1897 L. Levaggi Building, now a saloon and restaurant. In true Old West fashion, the bathrooms are outside. They do, however, flush.

The bar's ceiling has hundreds of dollar bills attached to it along with each donor's business card. To participate, you put a thumb tack through the bill and your card, and the bartender hands you a pole with a magnet on it. You can put the dollar anywhere on the ceiling. It astonishes me, even galls me, the way people will throw their money away on such frivolous foolishness. (My dollar is on the ceiling near the north wall, between a beer sign and the stained glass transom over the front door, with my business card attached. I consider it an investment in advertising and will duly deduct the expense.)

Beyond the Levaggi Building is a two-story, clapboard hotel. East of it is an 1878 general store, the oldest continuously operating business in La Grange. Across the street from the store is an old tin-sided service station that brings back memories of the early days of automobile travel.

As State Route 132 heads east through town, it takes a bend to the south, but you should go straight instead to view three of La Grange's most historic buildings in a cluster just east of the highway. On the left you will see what appears to be a wooden building, but the wood is merely a false front for the oldest adobe building in La Grange. A sign states it was built prior to 1850 and later served as the post office and even later as a stable.

Opposite the stable is the Inman Building, which features a cut sandstone false front and rock walls, the first such structure in La Grange. John W. Inman and three fellow Missourians erected the building in 1850. Over the years it served as a trading post, store, garage, and post office. It is now a museum, open only on Sundays, with area memorabilia and new-old-stock merchandise. An adjoining room features a series of detailed models of La Grange's historic buildings.

East of the Inman Building stands the wooden Stanislaus County jail, built in 1900 to replace the 1858 original that burned to the ground. If you question the stoutness of a wooden jail, this one was built with the boards laid flat and stacked log-cabin style for strength.

To see more of La Grange, take the bend in the highway heading south and turn right immediately on Floto Road. On your right is the 1852 St. Louis Mission, erected by French sailors who jumped ship in San Francisco to join the Gold Rush. Despite its history, I could find no graves of natives of France, although I did discover headstones mentioning Portugal, Ireland, Mexico, and "Chili."

The Levaggi Building in La Grange features an ornate bar and mirror brought from Hornitos and hundreds of dollar bills tacked to the ceiling.

Across the street from the mission stands the 1874 schoolhouse and, beyond it, the La Grange Cemetery. You have been on Floto Road, and in this cemetery are the graves of German-born William Floto, who died in 1871, and his wife Addie. In this graveyard I did find one Frenchman, a native of Bordeaux.

In the west end of the La Grange Cemetery is a marker worth seeking out. In a brick-walled space is the headstone, now lying flat in concrete, of Nancy Kennan. A carved monument behind the grave explains that she came to La Grange in 1854 by covered wagon as a fifty-eight-year-old widow. What is unusual about this headstone is her birth date. Most people who entered the Gold Rush were young, so it is quite rare to view a California stone of someone born in 1796.

A third cemetery, one mile west of town on State Route 132, has several graves of Frenchmen, along with natives of Italy, Switzerland, Canada, and England. Farther west of town is extensive evidence of dredging operations along the Tuolumne River.

When You Go

La Grange is 24 miles northwest of Hornitos. From Hornitos, take County Road J16 (Hornitos Road) west for 7.4 miles. Turn left as J16 becomes Merced Falls Road. Follow that road for 5.7 miles, where you will turn right on County Road J59 (La Grange Road) and proceed north for 10.4 miles. Turn right on State Route 132 and go .5 of a mile east to La Grange.

La Grange is also 31 miles east of Modesto and 25 miles west of Coulterville on State Route 132.

The grave of Portuguese-born Joao Maria stands near the 1852 St. Louis Mission, the first church in Stanislaus County.

Chapter Two

GHOSTS OF THE NORTHERN MINES

Main photo: *The office of the Empire Mine Superintendent George Starr contains ore specimens and a secure-looking safe made in Los Angeles.*

Inset photo: *A rock used by miners for core-drilling contests sits in Forest City. Along with drills and other mining equipment stands a blade of a two-man saw, a reminder that Forest City became a lumber center after its mining days.*

Despite the fame of the Mother Lode, the greatest concentration of lode gold came from an area north of Auburn, a place referred to by miners as the "Northern Mines." The richest of those mines, located in Nevada County, were not the small-time workings of hardy prospectors but rather the province of investors with deep pockets and owners with enormous capital at stake. These mines were among the longest-lasting, biggest-producing mines in California. Nevada County, with $440 million, produced more than twice as much gold between 1848 and 1965 as any other California county.

The Grass Valley Area

Grass Valley, twenty-five miles north of Auburn, has an historic downtown business district filled with Gold Rush–era buildings. Unfortunately, it is also filled with people and automobiles. Like several larger towns in chapter one, Grass Valley simply is too much of this century and not enough of the nineteenth for inclusion in this book. Nevertheless, I recommend walking its downtown area (a free tour booklet is widely available). The town's star attraction is the Empire Mine State Park (see pages 66–67).

Nevada City

When an unknown prospector found placer gold where Nevada City would later stand, he named his spot Deer Creek Dry Diggings. Later it would be called Caldwell's Upper Store for Dr. A. B. Caldwell's trading post. Finally it became Nevada and then, when it was incorporated in 1851, City of Nevada. By 1858 it was widely known as Nevada City.

Nevada City likely provided the name for California's eastern neighbor, as Nevada territory was named in 1861, long after Nevada City was already a thriving community. Furthermore, the Washoe silver rush was started by Nevada City miners who had ventured east over the Sierra Nevada and brought back ore samples. When "Nevada" was finalized for the new state, Nevada City residents protested, saying they had the name first.

According to the 1850 census, Nevada City had a population of 1,067. But by the

Nevada City women staged a grand ball to raise money for the construction of Pennsylvania Engine Co. No. 2, which was finished in 1861.

end of that year, it had risen to 6,000 citizens as miners flocked to an area where gold veins did not pinch out as usual but rather widened into remarkable primary deposits. Miners would burrow into the hills, in a process that became known as "coyoteing" after the digging prowess of that canine.

The town's population rose to 10,000 by the late 1850s, when Nevada City was "Queen of the Northern Mines" and the third-largest California city. But by the end of the decade, Nevada City was already in decline, with many prospectors heading east to the silver excitement of the Nevada Territory's Comstock Lode.

Walking and Driving Around Nevada City

Nevada City's entire downtown business section is a national historic district. The primary street to explore is Broad Street, but a good place to start a walking tour is at the Chamber of Commerce, located one block north of

Assay kits were used at Grass Valley mines to determine the value of ore samples.

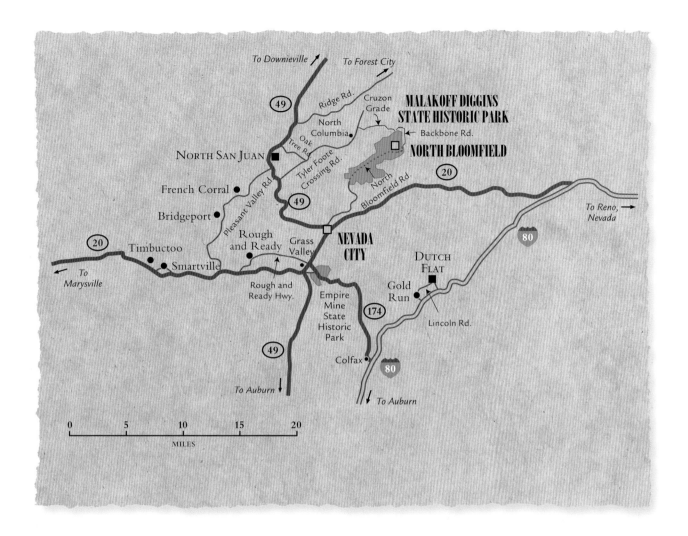

Broad Street where Commercial, Main, Union, and Coyote streets all converge. There you can obtain a free walking-tour guide.

A logical second stop is a few doors northwest on Main at the 1861 Nevada Hose Company No.1, a graceful two-story structure with delicate carpenter's lace gingerbread trim. It houses a museum that contains many Native American baskets and tools, a large display of Chinese artifacts, and an eclectic assortment of household items.

On Broad Street you will find the largest concentration of interesting buildings, beginning with the 1856–57 National Hotel, an elegant amalgamation of three three-story brick buildings on the east end of the business district. Up the street stands the 1859 Nevada Theater. Across the street are the 1861 Firehouse No. 1 and the 1880s New York Hotel, now a series of shops.

The lovely 1864 Methodist Church stands where Broad Street begins a turn to the northwest, and beyond the church .3 of a mile is St. Canice Catholic Cemetery, which contains excellent marble headstones, many for natives of Ireland and Italy.

Immediately south of that graveyard is the 1851 Pioneer Cemetery. The tallest marker gave me chills of admiration. It is for Henry Meredith, born in Virginia in 1826. He died in a battle at Pyramid Lake, Utah Territory (now Nevada), in 1860. His epitaph reads, "Brave, gifted, generous, and faithful, he closed a life of usefulness and purity by a death of honor." What created the chills were his last words, also on the marker: "No. Leave me here. I'm going to put you in peril." Wounded, he said this to others, resisting the aid of those who offered to help him from the field.

When You Go

Nevada City is 4 miles north of Grass Valley on Highway 49 and State Route 20.

Nevada City's National Hotel claims to be the oldest continuously operated in California. Construction began in 1856 and was completed the next year.

The Nevada Theater featured performances by such notables as Mark Twain and Jack London.

The Grass Valley Loop

A full day's loop from Grass Valley features eight mining sites, concluding with North Bloomfield, a lovely Northern Mine community, and the Malakoff Diggins, the eerie site of an environmental disaster.

Rough and Ready

In Wisconsin in the fall of 1849 a group of would-be miners formed the Rough and Ready Mining Company and headed west with "Rough and Ready" painted on their wagons. Their leader, Captain A. A. ("Cappy") Townsend, had served with General Zachary ("Old Rough and Ready") Taylor in the Mexican War. When they found gold and established a camp, its name was a foregone conclusion. Townsend and his group mined $40,000 in placer gold before the spring of 1850.

In that same year, some of the miners, unhappy about a federal mining tax, held a meeting to prepare articles of secession from the United States and to declare the Republic of Rough and Ready. The self-declared "republic" lasted from April until July 4, an appropriate day to "rejoin" the country. Ironically, the president of the United States during that "secession" was "Old Rough and Ready" himself, although he died five days after the Fourth of July.

When placer deposits were depleted by about 1855, hydraulic mining was attempted in the area, but the effort failed because of insufficient water.

One of the most photogenic buildings in Rough and Ready today is the old I.O.O.F. Hall, now a community center, which stands, partially hidden in foliage, on the north side of the road on the west end of town. East of the hall along the highway is the weathered W. H. Fippen General Blacksmith Building.

A plaque between the two buildings commemorates

the Rough and Ready secession. Nearby is a marble tablet "To Rough and Ready from the Republic of the Philippines." The marker is dated April 7, 1950, the centennial of the "secession." One wonders if the Philippine government, perhaps with its own thoughts of independence, was disparaging the United States with the tablet.

There used to be one more excellent historic building in town. Across the highway from Stage Coach Way, .2 of a mile east of the Fippen Building, is a dirt road that heads south a short distance to a replica of the Rough and Ready School, which burned in 1994. The building is a private residence.

To reach the town's small cemetery, turn north on Stage Coach Way and go .2 of a mile.

When You Go
Rough and Ready is 8 miles west of Grass Valley. Take the Marysville-Empire Street turnoff from Highway 49 and head west on State Route 20 for 5.4 miles. Turn northeast on Rough and Ready Highway and proceed 2.6 miles into town.

Smartville

James Smart built a hotel in 1856, and the town that grew there was named Smartsville for him. The post office dropped an "s" to become Smartville in 1867. In the 1870s, hydraulic mining created a gold bonanza, with about $13 million washed from the hills by 1879. At its height, Smartville had sixteen saloons and a population of about 1,500. The town went into decline after 1883.

Smartville's cemetery is on State Route 20 between the two intersections of Smartville Road. Continue west through town to the highway and turn left. The turnoff to the cemetery is .7 of a mile east on the south side of the road. There you will find about seventy-five graves, with several of the headstones spelling the town's name "Smartsville."

When You Go
From Rough and Ready, return on Rough and Ready Highway southwest to State Route 20 and turn right. Continue for 6.9 miles, where a right turn on Smartville Road takes you into town in .6 of a mile.

Timbuctoo

Timbuctoo is a very minor site, but since you are nearby, you should take a look. Besides, you will honestly be able to claim that you have circled the globe as far as Timbuctoo.

The only reminder of the town is the ruins of the 1855 Wells Fargo Office and Stewart Brothers Store that lie on the right side of the road about .6 of a mile from State Route 20.

Empire Mine State Historic Park

The Empire Mine is a fine place to learn about the fundamentals of the mining process. You can peer down the Empire shaft, which drops almost a mile into the earth. You can tour the machine shop, which has an array of tools and the smell of oil and metal. You can walk through the mine company offices, where officials watched over the ore extracted from Grass Valley's richest mine, which operated from 1850 until 1956 and produced, at today's prices, more than $2 billion in gold.

You can also view the rewards of that successful mining operation by touring the Bourne "Cottage," an opulent home most people would consider a mansion. One treat at the Bourne Cottage occurs on weekends from spring until fall, when historical recreations of scenes from the mine owners' lives are presented.

As an added attraction, within a year or two of the publication of this book, you will be able to take an electric mine train tour into the Empire itself.

To visit the Empire Mine, leave Highway 49 at the Marysville/Empire Street exit. Follow Empire Street east to the park entrance, a distance of 1.3 miles.

Above: *The 1897 Bourne "Cottage" was so called because the Bourne family, who owned the Empire Mine, had several other larger homes.*

Right: *The Empire Mine's Machine Shop contains an amazing array of tools—and a pin-up girl.*

Facing page: *Ore and miners were hauled up by cables through the Empire Shaft, but the mules who brought the ore through the mine's tunnels to this shaft lived their lives underground.*

Rough and Ready's Fippen Blacksmith Shop was notable because it reportedly was where singer, dancer, and actress Lotta Crabtree gave her very first performance at the age of six.

North Star Mining Museum

A second excellent Grass Valley attraction is the North Star Mining Museum, which contains some of California's best mining memorabilia. A collection of gold ore from throughout the Mother Lode is one highlight. One of the museum's more unusual acquisitions is an 1899 dynamite packing machine.

But its most dramatic attraction is a huge Pelton wheel, the largest in the world when it was installed at the former powerhouse in 1896. A Pelton wheel utilizes the force of a turbine-directed jet of water to turn buckets on the periphery of the wheel to produce electric power. It was named for inventor Lester A. Pelton, who patented the device in 1880.

To visit the North Star Mining Museum from the Empire Mine, return on Empire Street west to Highway 49, cross the freeway, and take an immediate right turn, which will double back under the highway as Allison Ranch Road. The museum will be in front of you across Courtney Street.

Both photos: *Smartville's sole building of note is the 1871 Church of the Immaculate Conception. A local resident said that it has not been used since at least the 1960s, and it shows.*

Given the sparse remains, you may find it difficult to imagine that Timbuctoo, supposedly named for or by an African miner from Timbuktu, once was the largest town in eastern Yuba County. Originally a placer site, the community prospered with hydraulic mining in 1854 and featured a theater, a church, hotels, saloons, and other businesses. It died when hydraulicking was effectively outlawed in 1884 (see the North Bloomfield entry, page 72, for details).

When You Go

Timbuctoo is northwest of Smartville. Follow Smartville Road west .5 of a mile back to State Route 20. Then turn right in .2 of a mile onto a one-lane plank bridge that leads you to Timbuctoo in .7 of a mile.

Bridgeport

The tiny site of Bridgeport features one of northern California's most beautiful engineering wonders: the nation's longest single-span wooden covered bridge.

Urias and Manuel Nye opened a trading post at a logical crossing of the South Fork of the Yuba River in 1849. The spot became known as Nyes Landing. A toll bridge was in place by 1851, supplanted in 1862 by the remarkable 232-foot covered bridge that stands today. Because the Yuba had been "bridged," the community was no longer a "landing," and Nyes Landing became Bridgeport.

By the 1920s, Bridgeport was not so much a community as a ranch and a tourist attraction, the latter called the Kneebone Pleasure Resort. The resort featured a store, rental cabins, a dance pavilion, and picnic facilities. The main attraction, however, was the river and its sandy beaches.

Today, river outings are still enormously popular. When I went to Bridgeport on a weekend to hear a talk about the bridge (given on Saturdays and Sundays at 11 A.M. and 2 P.M.), the parking lot was jammed. The river was filled with families enjoying the cool water.

The covered bridge at Bridgeport is even more dramatic and graceful than the much longer one at Knights Ferry (see chapter one), perhaps because it is a single span. Plaques near the entrance provide details of the construction of the bridge, which afforded an essential river crossing for the Virginia Turnpike Company Toll Road. The road was part of a system that connected Marysville, California, and Virginia City, Nevada, serving both the Northern Mines and the Comstock Lode.

In addition to its wonderful bridge, Bridgeport features a barn and a 1950s-era home, now a visitors' center.

When you view Bridgeport's marvelous covered bridge from the highway that now bypasses it, the bridge looks as if it cannot conceivably span the distance it does, rather like an airborne long jumper covering seemingly impossible territory.

Southwest of the visitors' center about 700 feet is the Kneebone Family Cemetery. Buried there are members of three pioneer families of Bridgeport—the Thompsons, Coles, and Kneebones. A brochure available at the visitors' center provides interesting family histories.

When You Go

From Smartville, return to State Route 20 and head east back toward Rough and Ready. Turn north in 1.5 miles onto Pleasant Valley Road and follow it 7.6 miles to Bridgeport.

French Corral

In 1849, a French settler reportedly built a stock pen for his mules, providing a name for the camp that would develop when placer deposits were found in 1851 or 1852. At its peak, French Corral had a population estimated at 3,800. Placer mining gave way to hydraulic mining, which lasted until it was effectively prohibited in 1884.

If you are coming from Bridgeport on Pleasant Valley Road, you will arrive at the French Corral Cemetery before you reach the tiny community itself. The dirt road leading to the cemetery is on the left side of the road next to a mailbox with the address 19881. The cemetery has about fifty graves, many of them recent. The older graves are near the entrance, where I found natives of France and the Isle of Man. The oldest headstone I located was from 1865.

French Corral is .2 of a mile beyond the cemetery. The only building of note is the 1853 brick Wells Fargo Office.

Beyond that brick building is a marker commemorating the first long distance telephone in the world. The Ridge Telephone Company erected a line in 1877 that connected French Corral's hydraulic operation, the

The Wells Fargo Office in French Corral is constructed in the classic Mother Lode style with an overhanging porch and heavy iron doors.

Milton Mining and Water Company, with its offices at its French Lake water source, fifty-eight miles to the northeast. The line went through North San Juan (below) and North Bloomfield (page 72) en route.

When You Go

French Corral is 2.6 miles northeast of Bridgeport on Pleasant Valley Road. Note hydraulic mining's environmental effects between Bridgeport and French Corral.

North San Juan

Rich placer deposits were discovered around North San Juan in 1853. One of the first prospectors, a Mexican-American War veteran, called a nearby mound San Juan Hill for one in Mexico named San Juan de Ulloa. The mining camp took the name of the hill, and when a post office was granted in 1857, "north" was added because another San Juan already existed in California.

A 300-mile-long flume, completed in 1859, brought water from reservoirs in the Sierra Nevada to North San Juan, which allowed hydraulic mining to flourish in the North San Juan Ridge, part of an ancient channel of the Yuba River.

During the 1870s, the population of North San Juan rose to as many as 10,000 citizens, and several hydraulic operations had their headquarters in town. The flume actually passed over what is now Highway 49.

Walking and Driving Around North San Juan

The first building of North San Juan that you will see coming from the south is the 1923 former school, now a community center, on the west side of the road. It last had students in 1984. Earlier schools have stood on the site since 1868.

As you enter downtown North San Juan, on your left are two attached brick buildings from about 1860. The first structure reportedly was a print shop, while the larger building was a grocery store with its own meat market and hardware department. It was later "remodeled," if that is the right word, when it lost a small second story and had its front gutted to create an auto mechanic's garage.

Across the highway from the garage is Cemetery Alley, which takes you up to the Protestant Cemetery, the prettiest graveyard in the Grass Valley Loop. Many of the graves are for natives of Wales. I liked the sentiment of the epitaph for John E. Fuller, who died in 1890 at age fifty-seven: "To live in hearts we leave behind is not to die."

Up the street from the garage is a string of historic buildings, including the 1853 two-story Bigley's Market. On the north end of the block is the 1854 Wells Fargo Building, which later served various commercial purposes.

A left turn on Flume Street, beyond the Wells Fargo Building, takes you to the lovely 1856 United Methodist Church, which, according to a sign, is "one of the oldest of its faith in continuous operation in California."

One block southeast of the highway, on Cherokee Street, stands a large brick ruin, obscured by overgrowth, of one of four Victorian homes that burned in 1982.

North of downtown North San Juan .2 of a mile, just beyond Oak Tree Road, is the Catholic Cemetery on a knoll east of the highway. Its attractive black and silver wrought-iron gate is visible from Highway 49.

When You Go

From French Corral, continue northeast on Pleasant Valley Road for 4.2 miles to Highway 49. North San Juan is 2.4 miles north of that junction.

North Bloomfield and Malakoff Diggins State Historic Park

North Bloomfield is the premier ghost town of the Northern Mines. Now a state historic park, it moves at a much slower pace than the other three more famous state park mining towns—Coloma, Columbia, and Bodie. Some Gold Country tour books consider North Bloomfield a "side trip." Not so—it is *the* destination.

Early prospectors in the North Bloomfield area were disappointed in their findings along a stream and so named it Humbug Creek. When a camp formed nevertheless, the community was called Humbug. Despite the moniker, the town prospered. When a post office was granted, the town was hardly a "humbug," and citizens chose the name Bloomfield. The Postal Service required the addition of "North," as they did with North San Juan, because another Bloomfield already existed in California.

The reason the camp went from a "humbug" to a town of 2,000 citizens was the invention of hydraulic mining. In 1853 local prospector Edward Matteson used a rawhide hose and a wooden nozzle to wash gold-laden ore from a bluff. Matteson's invention drastically changed the gold mining industry. His wooden nozzle was refined into a metal cannon-like contraption called a "monitor" or "giant" that propelled water with incredible force into gravel banks containing gold. The gold was exposed and separated, while the water, which eventually was brought to North Bloomfield through forty-three miles of flumes and ditches, washed away the waste.

As a result, gold that had been impenetrably locked in gravel became highly profitable to mine. An estimated $4.5 million in gold was retrieved from only two of the area's many mines. At one of them, the Malakoff, gold was smelted on site. The largest bar weighed 510 pounds

The 1856 United Methodist Church in North San Juan was spared in each of three major fires that virtually destroyed the town.

and was valued at $114,000, the bar of greatest value ever shipped from Nevada County.

The process was almost too easy—if it had not been for hydraulicking's aftereffects. The mines themselves were denuded of vegetation, and downstream from the mines enormous amounts of waterborne detritus created environmental havoc: Silt in rivers caused floods, killed fish and riparian wildlife, destroyed farmlands, and hampered navigation as far away as San Francisco Bay.

For ten years, concerned Californians waged a legal battle against powerful financial interests to halt the devastation. In 1884 a federal court finally ordered a halt to the wholesale dumping of tailings, effectively eliminating most hydraulic mining—and effectively emptying North Bloomfield.

Walking and Driving Around North Bloomfield

North Bloomfield today is a picturesque town of picket fences, shade trees, small but pleasant single-story clapboard homes, and several attractive wood-frame commercial buildings.

The state park headquarters is Cummins Hall—a former dance hall and saloon containing a well-stocked museum and an informative video on hydraulic mining.

Next door is the reconstructed Kallenberger Barber Shop, and, beyond, the tiny King's Saloon, built in the

North Bloomfield contains many original buildings, but this is a faithful reconstruction of the 1870s Smith and Knotwell Drugstore, which had a Masonic Lodge upstairs. The first floor contains many authentic items.

Above: *The McKillican and Mobley General Store was a social center for North Bloomfield. It also had the post office, which closed in 1941.*

Right: *The 556-foot Hiller Tunnel helped drain the waste of the Malakoff Diggins's hydraulic operations.*

Facing page: *If the Malakoff Diggins were natural, we'd think it was beautiful, because it has an otherworldly appearance, resembling Utah's Bryce Canyon. We are reminded that this is unnatural, however, by a stream running through the diggins with water disturbingly darker than it should be.*

early 1870s. Next door is a reconstruction of the two-story Masonic Lodge with the Smith and Knotwell Drugstore on its first floor.

Across the street is the 1870 McKillican and Mobley General Store. It contains new-old-stock items and the town's post office, with a convenient outdoor mail drop.

West of town .4 of a mile is the 1860 St. Columncille's Catholic Church. It originally was located northeast of French Corral, where it first served as the Bridgeport Union Guard Hall before becoming a church in 1869. It was moved to this location, the site of an earlier Catholic church, in 1971.

Next door to St. Columncille's is the 1872 North Bloomfield School, a large, two-room L-shaped building that allowed for a teacher's nightmare: About forty desks are set up in one of the rooms. The school last had students in 1941.

Behind the church is a small, well-kept cemetery. Across the street from the church is a path that takes you a short distance through a manzanita grove to an overlook of the Le Du hydraulic mine.

But that view pales in comparison to the sight that awaits you .4 of mile west of the church and school at the Malakoff Diggins. Park your car and take the 240-foot trail to the overlook.

A five-minute walk beyond that overlook gives you an even better view of the "diggins." The colors of the denuded hills range from slate gray to tan to tawny brown.

Beyond the main diggins site .2 of a mile on North Bloomfield Road is the West Point Overlook, where a short hike takes you down to a water pipe and its monitor. This short but somewhat steep trail goes into the mine itself, giving you a genuine feel for how the hydraulicking process can alter the environment.

When You Go
North Bloomfield is 15 miles northeast of North San Juan. Drive north on Highway 49 for .2 of a mile and turn right onto Oak Tree Road. In 2.7 miles, turn left on Tyler Foote Crossing Road and follow it for 4.5 miles to the small community of North Columbia (note its lovely former schoolhouse). In 1.5 miles beyond North Columbia, turn right onto Cruzon Grade (it becomes the main road and Tyler Foote Crossing the lesser). Cruzon Grade will dovetail into Backbone Road. In 5.7 miles from North Columbia, turn right on Derbec Road, which in .7 of a mile will meet North Bloomfield Road. Turn right and proceed 1.3 miles to North Bloomfield.

From North Bloomfield, you can return by a 15-mile direct route to Nevada City via North Bloomfield Road. It is twisting, winding, and narrow, and 5.4 miles of it is

Gold Run's 1855 Pioneer Union Church, which was built by contributions from miners, is still used on Sundays. Note the church's shingle siding, which is rather rare in Gold Rush country.

unpaved. If you love the back roads, you will relish this drive, which includes a dramatic view from a one-lane bridge over the South Yuba River.

Gold Run and Dutch Flat

Gold Run and Dutch Flat are not a part of the Grass Valley Loop but rather a separate, inviting secondary trip from Grass Valley. You will travel through Colfax en route, which has a delightful downtown fronting the railroad tracks.

Gold Run
Mountain Springs was the name founder O. W. Hollenbeck gave this now-peaceful former mining town in 1854 after placer deposits were discovered along Gold Run Canyon.

The town's name was changed to Gold Run in 1863, about the time that hydraulicking began. Between 1865 and 1878, more than $6 million in gold was shipped from the Gold Run Express Office. The court decision curtailing hydraulic mining led to the decline of Gold

The former Dutch Flat School contains two classrooms on the first floor and an auditorium on the second. The Towle Company used the railroad car to store construction materials when they rebuilt the school after a fire.

Run beginning in 1884, but there was moderate activity until 1915. Dredging occurred in the 1920s and 1930s on a limited scale.

When you leave Interstate 80 to head to present-day Gold Run, you will cross over the highway and immediately come to a "T." At the northeast corner of that intersection stands the 1855 Pioneer Union Church.

After visiting the church, continue north for .3 of a mile on Gold Run Road to the main part of town. There you will find the Gold Run Store, closed and boarded at this writing, and a modern post office.

To see Gold Run's best building, turn left (west) on Lincoln Road and cross the railroad tracks. Turn left immediately onto Gold Run School Road, which in .6 of a mile dead ends at the lovely schoolhouse, now a private residence.

Dutch Flat

Dutch Flat seems like an ideal place to live. Although it is easily accessible to large communities via the interstate, it truly resides in its past. At an elevation of 3,144 feet, it is cooler than many of the sites in Gold Country but is also low enough to avoid a serious winter. Furthermore, Dutch Flat, unlike many Gold Rush camps, never had a major fire, so it remains a lovely, well-preserved nineteenth-century town.

German prospectors and merchants Charles and Joseph Dornbach began placer mining here in 1851 and called the place Dutch Charlie's Flat. The name was shortened to Dutch Flat when the town received its post office in 1856. When hydraulic mining began in 1857, the community's population grew to about 2,000 citizens; in 1860 the town had the largest number of voters in Placer County. When the Central Pacific Railroad was being constructed, as many as 2,000 Chinese also lived in Dutch Flat, but they naturally moved on as the railroad progressed. The town was well known during the 1860s because the Central Pacific called their chosen path for the transcontinental railroad the "Dutch Flat Route."

By 1867, forty-five hydraulic mines were operating within a mile and a half of town. It also was the first location in which newly invented dynamite was extensively utilized in mining.

Like many other Northern Mine towns, Dutch Flat's prosperous times ended when hydraulicking was virtually halted in 1884, but not before producing an estimated $5 million in gold.

Walking and Driving Around Dutch Flat

As you approach Dutch Flat, you will enter a lovely valley with several pleasant homes (and no "flat" to be seen). When you turn onto Main Street, you enter into a beautiful, quiet town that features several excellent historic buildings shaded by poplar and locust trees. On your left is the 1858 two-story I.O.O.F. Hall. The lower floor contained H. R. Hudepohl's store.

Next door is the 1856 Masonic Lodge. Across the street from the lodge is the three-story Dutch Flat Hotel, which at this writing has been for sale for several years. It is falling into disrepair, and one hopes a buyer comes along to restore it. It was built in 1852 as a one-story hotel.

Across the street from the hotel is the stone 1854 Dutch Flat Trading Post and the post office.

A half-mile walk (or drive) takes you to Dutch Flat's two attractive cemeteries. Go north on Main to Fifth Avenue, turn right, and then turn left onto Cemetery Road. The first graveyard is the public one, which sits underneath a canopy of trees and within a carpet of lush ferns.

You can walk through the northeast exit of the public cemetery to the Masonic and I.O.O.F. cemeteries, which are side by side up the road. The largest marker is for German-born Herman R. Hudepohl (1828–1896), the

Dutch Flat offers a study in building materials: On the left stands Dutch Flat's stone-block I.O.O.F. Hall, which has tin covering its side walls; in the middle is the Masonic Lodge, which has a stone first floor and a clapboard second story; on the right is a wooden false-front commercial building.

man who had the store beneath the I.O.O.F. Hall. Incidentally, he played no favorites—he was a Mason as well as an Odd Fellow.

As you return on Cemetery Street to Fifth Avenue, you can see the rear of one of Dutch Flat's most elegant buildings, the Methodist Episcopal Church. To visit it, turn left on Fifth and left again on Stockton. The wood-frame church, which was begun in 1859 and completed in 1861 and is still in use, has more ornate carving on its face and steeple than most churches in Gold Rush Country.

Directly across from the church is another gem, the former Dutch Flat School, now a community center.

You passed another historic building as you were entering town, but it was very easy to miss, so you can examine it as you leave Dutch Flat. Continue on Stockton past the school as the street turns south and inter-

sects with Sacramento, your street into town. This time turn left. Almost immediately on your left will be an 1870 Chinese store, which, like the Chew Kee Store in Fiddletown, is made of solid adobe, not adobe bricks.

When you leave Dutch Flat and return to Ridge Road, this time go onto Interstate 80 heading west and get off almost immediately at the rest area, which is built on the site of one of the Gold Run Mining District's major hydraulic operations, the Stewart Mine. At the rest area are several informative plaques and a hydraulic monitor.

When You Go

From Grass Valley, take State Route 174 southeast for about 12 miles to Colfax. Take I-80 east (actually northeast) for 8 miles and exit at Gold Run.

Turn left on Magra Road. (Important note: Do not be confused by a sign that implies that Gold Run is to the right. It directs you only to a historical plaque, not

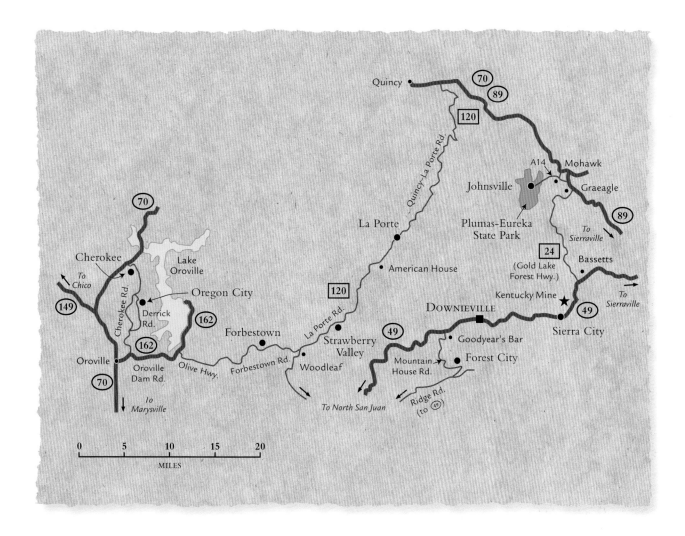

the town itself.) Cross the interstate and turn right at the stop sign.

Dutch Flat is 3 miles northwest of Gold Run. From Gold Run, go north on Lincoln Road for 1.7 miles to Ridge Road (about half way along the route, look for desolate evidence of hydraulic mining on your left). Turn left on Ridge, and, in .2 of a mile, turn left again onto Sacramento Street, which will take you into downtown Dutch Flat in .9 of a mile.

The Oroville Area

The mining camps that extend north and east from Oroville are not as dramatic or complete as those near Grass Valley. With the exception of charming Downieville,

this area is for the purist who does not require extensive historic remains.

Oregon City and Cherokee

Oregon City

Oregon City was founded by Oregonians in the fall of 1848. By 1859 four mills with a total of thirty-two stamps were processing between ten and eighteen tons of ore daily, but the town eventually faded into obscurity.

Oregon City features a small covered bridge and an 1877 schoolhouse. Beyond the town's school is the cemetery. The lane leading to it begins immediately beyond the fence line for a residence with 2042 on the mailbox. Perhaps fifty to seventy-five graves are within the cemetery, including headstones for natives of Germany, Wales, and Scotland.

Cherokee

After leaving Oregon City, you will arrive at the Cherokee Cemetery one-half mile before you reach the town itself. Inscribed at the entrance are several Bible verses, including, appropriately, from I Timothy: "For we brought nothing into this world, and it is certain we can carry nothing out." The older headstones are in the back of the cemetery, including markers for natives of Wales and Portugal.

Cherokee itself is made up of the former school, now a private residence; the old post office; the large rock ruin of the Spring Valley Mine and Assay Office, with its stone vault; and a wood building that is now the Cherokee Land Office, Museum, and Store. Nearby is a monument and plaque dedicated in 1967 with the cooperation of the Cherokee Nation, DeBeers Consolidated Mines, and others.

The unusual cooperation of a Native American nation and a South African diamond company requires an explanation: The community was founded in 1850 by young Cherokee gold seekers, reportedly led by their New England schoolmaster. It is also one of the few places in California where genuine diamonds were found, although in very limited quantity and mostly of industrial quality only.

The primary allure of Cherokee, however, was gold, not diamonds. Hydraulic mining flourished from 1858 until the mid-1880s, producing an estimated $10 million in gold. Mining continued on a limited basis until 1944.

The plaque mentions that the first stores were erected by Welshmen in 1853, and that by 1875, during its hydraulicking bonanza, Cherokee had more than 1,000 citizens, who enjoyed seventeen saloons, eight hotels, three lodges, two churches, a brewery, and a theater. The plaque's pedestal is made up of interesting placer specimens, diamond ore, and stones from Oklahoma's Cherokee Nation.

If you drive beyond Cherokee, you can see dramatic scars from the hydraulic mining done nearby.

When You Go

From Oroville, head north on Cherokee Road for 6.5 miles and turn right on Derrick Road. Oregon City is .5 of a mile southeast.

Cherokee is 3.8 miles north of the intersection of

The principal attraction north of Oroville is Oregon City's attractive little covered bridge, a 1982 replica of an earlier bridge, which ushers you to a tidy 1877 schoolhouse, in service until 1922.

Cherokee Road and Derrick Road, the turnoff to Oregon City. You can return to Oroville the same way you came or continue past Cherokee to State Route 70, which joins State Route 149 back to Oroville.

Forbestown, Strawberry Valley, and La Porte

Forbestown

Wisconsin native Ben F. Forbes opened a general merchandise store in 1850 to serve local prospectors. By the time a post office was granted in 1854, it was for Forbestown.

The town reached a population of about 900 by 1855. Both placer and quartz mining were successful, with the biggest producer being the Gold Bank Mine, which yielded $2 million in gold between 1888 and 1904. Some mining continued into the 1930s, but in that same decade Forbestown was described as "a ghost town of heaped debris, old foundations, and crumbling structures with fallen roofs."

Even that debris has disappeared today. The only building of note in Forbestown is the 1857 Masonic Lodge and I.O.O.F. Hall. Along the west side of the building is Cemetery Lane. Leave your vehicle and walk along the lane, which appears to be a driveway but is not. You will reach the cemetery in a few dozen steps.

Strawberry Valley

Named for its proliferation of wild strawberries, Strawberry Valley was first placer mined in 1850. By 1852 the community had five or six houses, and three years later a post office was granted. The town became a supply center for area mines.

As you approach the tiny hamlet of Strawberry Valley on LaPorte Road, you'll see a highway sign announcing it. Immediately beyond that sign, take a right turn to the still-used Strawberry Valley Cemetery. In this cemetery I saw my last name for the only time in Gold Country on headstones for Boston native Joshua A. Varney (1802–1887) and his son of the same name, who died in 1898 at age sixty. His son's epitaph establishes that "We will meet in heaven."

Downtown Strawberry Valley is .4 of a mile beyond the cemetery. One building of interest is the large, wooden,

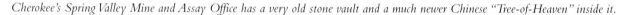

Cherokee's Spring Valley Mine and Assay Office has a very old stone vault and a much newer Chinese "Tree-of-Heaven" inside it.

Above: *The Forbestown Cemetery sits on a gently sloping hill in comforting tree shade. It features a large number of carefully carved old stones, such as one for Elisha M. Thrasher, who was "Killed by the caving of a bank on South Feather River" in 1858, his twenty-ninth year.*

Left: *Forbestown's combination Masonic Lodge and I.O.O.F. Hall has a plaque rescued from the lodge at the now-all-but-vanished town of St. Louis.*

La Porte's Union Hotel was established in 1855, although the present building dates from about 1905.

three-and-a-half story Columbus House Hotel, built in 1900. Another historic structure is the Strawberry Valley General Store, beyond the hotel, which has been in continuous service since it opened in 1852.

La Porte

Prospectors began working nearby Rabbit Creek in 1850, and when a post office was established in 1855, it was for Rabbit Town. Apparently that name was not dignified enough for local banker Frank Everts. In 1857, the town was renamed La Porte, for his home town in Indiana.

La Porte was located in an extremely successful mining area. Fifty hydraulic companies were operating by 1857, and the La Porte Mining District yielded a remarkable $60 million in gold between 1855 and 1871.

La Porte today features the three-story Union Hotel. Up the street is the rock ruin of the Wells Fargo Building.

South of the hotel on Church Street stand two interesting wood residences. Church Street has no church, but it does lead south to the town cemetery. Two graves from the 1990s are of an infant and a child, reminders that not only in pioneer days do children die.

If you walk to the northwest end of the cemetery, there is a back gate leading to a schoolhouse, which is adjacent to pleasant Gibson Park.

When You Go

From Oroville, head east from State Route 70 on Oroville Dam Road, which is State Route 162. East of Oroville, Route 162 becomes Olive Highway. At 8.3 miles, turn right on Forbestown Road and follow it for 12.3 miles,

at which point you will turn left on Old Forbestown Road. There is only a street sign, and the turnoff appears rather suddenly. "Old" Forbestown is .5 of a mile down that road. You rejoin Forbestown Road in .7 of a mile beyond the townsite.

Strawberry Valley is 13 miles northeast of Forbestown. Continue east on Forbestown Road to the small community of Woodleaf. Turn left on La Porte Road, which is U.S. Forest Service Road 120 and County Road E21. La Porte is 12.3 miles northeast of Strawberry Valley on La Porte Road.

Johnsville and Plumas-Eureka State Park

Johnsville and Plumas-Eureka State Park are interrelated and adjacent to each other. Since the mine predates the town, I suggest visiting the state park (where the mine is located) first.

Plumas-Eureka State Park

A group of nine prospectors first panned in Jamison Creek, which flows through the present-day state park, in May 1851. After incredibly rich primary deposits were found by two of their group on nearby Gold Mountain (now Eureka Peak), they and other friends formed the Eureka Company, the first California corporation created for the purpose of mining.

For the next twenty years, several small operations worked deposits with varying degrees of success. The name of the camp for the mines was Jamison City, which had a peak population of about 200.

The real bonanza came in 1872, when a British group, the Sierra Buttes Gold Mining Company Limited, bought up a series of claims, brought in the latest equipment, and consolidated the workings into one large operation. The Plumas-Eureka was born.

The mine had more than paid for itself within ten years and continued profitably for another twenty years before it was sold. The last good year was in 1897, although sporadic mining attempts were made into the 1940s.

Walking Around Plumas-Eureka State Park

Begin your tour at the park headquarters and museum, housed in the former bunkhouse. A walking tour brochure takes you to the primary attraction, the huge 1878 Mohawk (later, the Plumas-Eureka) Mill, a forty-eight-stamp mill that is the equivalent of about a seven-story building. You can, however, go beyond the mill up a more rugged trail to tramway ruins, a powder house, and the Eureka Tunnel.

Southeast of the main area of the park 1.7 miles at the end of Jamison Mine Road are several buildings of the Jamison Mine, which opened in the late 1880s.

Johnsville

Johnsville was a company town erected in 1876 by the Sierra Buttes Company for their Plumas-Eureka Mine. Originally called Johnstown, it was named for William Johns, the well-respected manager of the Plumas-Eureka Mine. When a post office was granted in 1882, the name was changed to Johnsville.

The premier building is the 1908 two-story Johnsville Hotel. On the opposite side of the street stands the firehouse, rebuilt in 1967 to its 1908 appearance. All but a few of the town's residences are occupied, and most are nicely maintained.

At the north end of town is the cemetery, which has an amazing variety of birthplace countries, considering its small size: Natives of Greece, Ireland, Italy, Scotland, England, Switzerland, Austria, and Herzegovina are buried there. One notable grave is for Johnsville native John Redstreake (1911–1981), the "undefeated long-board snowshoe champion." The first organized races in the western hemisphere on skis, then called "snowshoes," were held in this area in 1861.

When You Go

From La Porte, drive northeast on Forest Service Road 120, the Quincy–La Porte Road, which will turn left toward Quincy in 1.8 miles after La Porte. The right turn is Johnsville Road, a more direct route to Johnsville, but a local resident advised against taking it. Road 120 ends,

28.7 miles northeast of La Porte, at State Routes 70 and 89. Turn right. In 18.6 miles you will see a sign directing you onto County Road A14 to the Plumas-Eureka State Park, now 4.6 miles away.

Sierra City

Beginning in 1850, miners tunneled into the Sierra Buttes, which rise dramatically behind Sierra City, following a quartz ledge. In 1852, those same buttes let loose an avalanche that destroyed the tiny community below. The town was rebuilt as the Sierra Buttes mines prospered.

Sierra City received its post office in 1864. In 1878, the town of 400 citizens shipped $288,000 in gold via Wells Fargo. The total production of the Sierra City mines is estimated at $30 million.

Walking and Driving Around Sierra City

If you are entering Sierra City from the east, coming from Johnsville, the first structure of note, the 1871 Busch and Heringlake Building, will appear on your right. Built of local brick by August A. Busch, it has been, according to a plaque, a residence, a general store, and the offices of both Wells Fargo and Western Union.

At this writing it is the Busch and Heringlake Country Inn, and inside is a magnificent old safe with "A. C. Busch" written in ornate gold letters. The safe, according to the present owner, held miners' gold until it could be transferred to Wells Fargo. Incidentally, the owner inquired of the St. Louis August Busch family to determine if Sierra City's August Busch was related to the famous brewer, but they replied he was not.

West of the Busch Building stands the 1863 Masonic Lodge on the corner of Butte and Main streets. Behind it on Butte is the 1879 Sierra City Community Methodist Church.

The cemetery is on the west end of Sierra City. Just as you are leaving town, look for Cemetery Lane, which heads off to the right. The cemetery stands on a steep hill and contains many ornate gravestones, shaded by oak and pine trees, for natives of England, Ireland, Scotland, France, Germany, Portugal, the Azores, Italy, Sweden, Norway, and Mexico.

As you return from the cemetery, before you reach the highway, turn left on Butte Street, which will take you past the St. Thomas Catholic Church.

When You Go

From Johnsville, retrace your route down County Road A14 past Mohawk. In 6.9 miles, turn right onto Forest Service Road 24, the Gold Lake Forest Highway. After 15.2 miles of remarkably scenic driving, you will arrive at Highway 49. Head west 5 miles to Sierra City. On the

Above: *The Johnsville Hotel, no longer in service, has ornamental tin siding.*

Right: *The Sierra City Community Methodist Church has an unusual octagonal belfry. Note also the attractively jigged ornamental design under the eaves.*

way, consider stopping at the Kentucky Mine, a mile east of town (see pages 86–87).

Downieville

The confluence of the Yuba and a then-unnamed river yielded placer gold in the fall of 1849. The settlement that grew at the discovery site was variously called Jim Crow Diggins, Washingtonville, Missouri Town, and The Forks. The community finally settled on the name Downieville for Scotsman William Downie, its leading citizen. On Christmas Day of that year, Downie, who had proclaimed himself a major, climbed onto a cabin roof armed with a flag and a pistol. The major later wrote, "I made a short speech, waved the flag, and fired a few shots and finished up by giving three cheers for the American Constitution." Merry Christmas!

By May of the next year, Downieville had fifteen hotels and gambling houses along with four butcher shops and four bakeries. By the next year, it had 5,000 citizens.

Placer mining yielded to quartz and even hydraulic mining, but the excitement was over by 1867. One exception was the Gold Bluff Mine, which was worked sporadically into the 1950s, producing about $1.5 million in gold.

Walking and Driving Around Downieville

You are going to like Downieville from the moment you arrive. When you enter town coming from Sierra City,

you slowly pass attractive residences, an 1850s Protestant church, and an 1864 Masonic Lodge—and then you stop to check traffic from the opposite direction, because the highway narrows for a one-lane bridge as you cross the Downie River. This is the only place I know that Highway 49 goes to one lane, and the effect is absolutely charming.

You then enter a town running at its own unhurried pace. When I was there one warm September weekday, the fire horn went off announcing high noon. A singer in front of a downtown bar, accompanying himself on guitar, stopped mid-line in "What a Day for a Daydream." Two men engaged in a spirited conversation outside the newspaper office halted. But one of the men's dog tugged on his leash and gave out a soulful howl. When the siren ceased, the singer resumed from the same line, the spirited conversation resumed, and the dog, exhausted from his howling protest, lay down on the sidewalk. Passersby avoided the dog by going into the street. The same thing probably happens in New York City all the time.

Downtown Downieville meets at Main and Commercial streets. On the southeast corner stands the 1852 Craycroft Building, a brick and stone structure with an overhanging porch. A plaque states the building was famous for its seventy-foot-long basement bar, made from a single rip-sawn board.

Across the street on Main stands another excellent

The Sierra County Historical Park and Museum (The Kentucky Mine)

The mill tour at the Sierra County Historical Park and Museum is a genuine treat. Most mills remaining in Gold Rush County were stripped for salvage. The Kentucky Mill is in virtually operable condition, making it extremely rare and well worth touring.

The Sierra County Historical Society now operates the Kentucky Mine. Its museum features mineral samples, mining and logging equipment, historical photographs, and Native American and Chinese artifacts.

The Kentucky Mine began gold production in 1853. A five-stamp mill built in the 1860s was increased to ten stamps in 1888.

Emil Loeffler and his son Dutch are responsible for the preservation of the mine and mill. They reopened the mine in 1920 after it had been closed for years. They built a new mill largely out of salvaged equipment and ran it until 1944, when Dutch was killed in an accident in the mine. The mine was last worked in 1953.

The Sierra County Historical Park and Museum is a mile east of Sierra City. If you are coming from Johnsville, you will arrive at the mine before you reach Sierra City. It is open Wednesday through Sunday from Memorial Day until the end of September.

A restored trestle leads ore cars to the huge mill at the Kentucky Mine, near Sierra City. The site is so complete that it is on the National Register of Historic Places.

According to an historic marker on Downieville's 1852 Mackerman Building, it has been a brewery, a drugstore, a meat market, and now is home to The Mountain Messenger.

antique structure, the 1852 Mackerman Building. Currently it houses the state's oldest weekly newspaper, *The Mountain Messenger*. Its wood false front is deceiving, because the building has three-foot-thick stone side walls and a four-foot-thick mud and brick ceiling.

Visible on a hill behind the Mackerman Building is the unusual steeple of the 1858 Immaculate Conception Catholic Church.

To reach the cemetery, only .6 of a mile from downtown, continue east on Main from Commercial and follow the road as it climbs through a neighborhood. Go straight past Pearl Street and turn left at Gold Bluff Road when Main drops to the right. The cemetery is on your left. A sign states that this graveyard, dating from around 1876, was the second burial ground in Downieville. An earlier cemetery was being "disturbed by greedy miners," so the graves were disinterred and brought to this site. The most elaborate stone, for L. Byington (1820–1886), has an angel—one assumes St. Peter—writing a new name in the eternal book.

For yet another Downieville historic spot, turn south from Main onto Nevada Street. You will cross a bridge and then come to the Sierra County Sheriff's Gallows, the site of the 1885 hanging of James O'Neill. That was the only time it was used, and that was the last legal execution in the county.

Above: *The 1874 Forest City School had two classrooms serving students into the 1930s. It originally had a covered porch over the front door.*

Facing page: *Forest City's Dance Hall was built after an 1883 fire and once had three stories, with a barber shop, saloon, and billiard hall on the first floor, a rubber-cushioned dance hall on the second, and an I.O.O.F. hall on the third. When the top two stories collapsed from snow, the dance floor was moved to the first floor.*

When You Go
Downieville is 12.3 miles west of Sierra City on Highway 49.

Forest City

Forest City was founded in the 1850s as Brownsville, then Elizaville. When it received a post office in 1854, it was for Forest City. The postal service dropped the word "City" in 1895, but residents never accepted the change.

Originally a mining camp, Forest City eventually turned to logging after a much bigger strike in nearby Allegheny nearly emptied the town. David Wood owned a local sawmill that supplied the Douglas fir timbers for the covered bridge at Bridgeport (see page 69).

If you are coming from Downieville, you will see the Forest City's Mountain House Cemetery before you have any glimpse of the town itself. It is only a tenth of a mile before Main Street in Forest City, but the town is around the bend.

The cemetery and its tall flagpole stand on a hill north of the road. Many of the headstones date from the 1870s and 1880s.

As you enter Forest City, the first building on your right is one of the town's most photogenic: the wooden dance hall. Main Street proceeds uphill past a series of buildings and residences, many with a company-town look.

At the end of Main, at School Street, there is a small building to the right with "FCH&LC" on it. One wonders if this tiny town actually had a hook and ladder company.

School Street is not paved, but a two-wheel-drive truck can get up the street, where you will see the old weather-worn wood-frame building that still has its bell in the belfry.

When You Go
From Downieville, head west on Highway 49 for 3.8 miles. Turn south on Mountain House Road, which will take you through the tiny community of Goodyears Bar. The road turns to dirt and winds its way through a dense forest up and out of the valley of the Yuba River. This road is perfectly fine for passenger cars, but it is a slow, twisting route for the 9.4 miles to Forest City (those 9.4 road miles cover only 4.1 air miles).

Chapter Three

GHOSTS
OF THE NORTH
COUNTRY

Main photo: *The ghostly brick ruins of Shasta include M. Jacobsen & Co. Clothing Building (right), the town's first brick structure, which dates from 1853.*

Inset photo: *An ore car sits a bit incongruously on the front porch of the French Gulch Hotel and Dining Room.*

Ghost towns fan out from Redding to the northernmost reaches of California. The area is rich in scenery, including the great Trinity, Salmon, and Klamath rivers and magnificent Mount Shasta and Lassen Peak. The ghost towns are definitely enhanced by these surroundings. Despite the relatively rural nature of this chapter, however, only one site, High Grade, is on an unpaved road.

The Redding Area

Shasta

Shasta is the principal reminder in northern California that gold was not found solely in the Mother Lode and the Northern Mines. The first gold discovery in Shasta County was made in March 1848 by Major Pierson B. Reading, who, with the help of Indians, washed out about $800 per day from placers along Clear Creek. The tent city that grew was originally called Reading's Diggings or Reading's Springs. The name was changed to Shasta City in 1850, and when the post office was established a year later, the name was shortened to Shasta, a corruption of the name of an Indian tribe.

Shasta developed into an important metropolis not only for its own gold but also because the town was the gateway both to gold-rich Trinity County and to the rapidly opening Oregon frontier. The main street became lined with businesses to outfit expeditions and crowded with mule trains to carry the goods across the rugged trails that led west and north.

In 1853, fire swept through town. To avoid a recurrence, merchants rebuilt with brick, giving Shasta the distinction of having the longest row of brick buildings in California. The permanence of the new business district indicated the optimism that the merchants felt for Shasta's future, and for a time it was justified. At their peak, the mines in Trinity and Siskiyou counties were producing as much as $100,000 in ore per week, much of it freighted through town. During the winter of 1854–55, an estimated 1,876 mules packed supplies through Shasta. One mule reportedly carried a 352-pound safe from Shasta to Weaverville and then proceeded to lie down and die.

The 1855 Shasta County Courthouse, now a museum, served as the courthouse from 1862 until 1888, when Shasta lost the county seat to Redding.

Shasta's Masonic Lodge was built in 1853 and is still in use. Its charter was brought westward by Peter Lassen, for whom Lassen Peak is named.

Both veteran and inexperienced prospectors depended upon books like The Mine Examiner and Prospector's Companion.

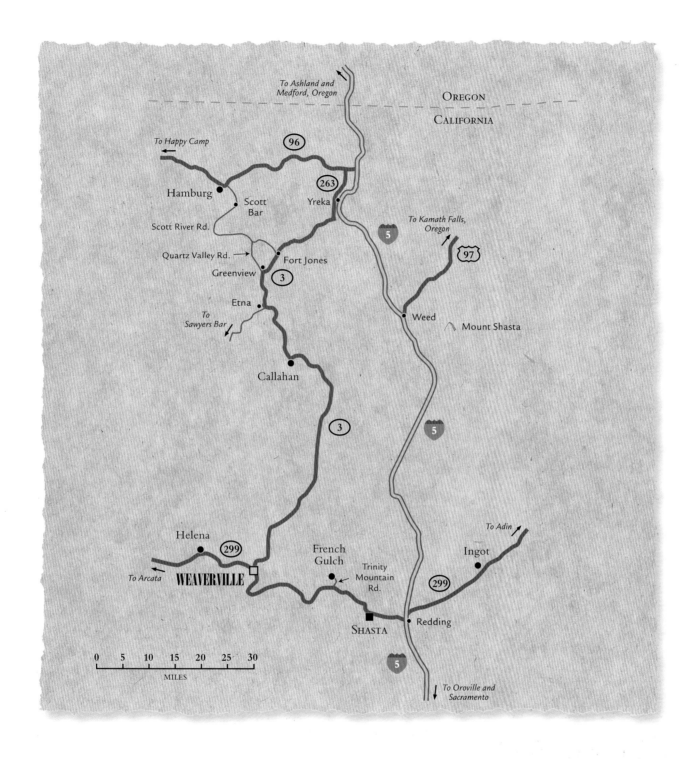

Shasta itself began to lie down and die in 1886, when the Central Pacific Railroad connecting San Francisco and Portland bypassed the town in favor of nearby Reading (later spelled "Redding" for R. B. Redding, a railroad land agent).

Walking and Driving Around Shasta

Shasta is now a California State Historic Park. Its street of brick buildings is still impressive, even though many have been reduced to mere walls and foundations. Start your visit at the former Shasta County Courthouse.

The courthouse features an art gallery with some lovely nineteenth-century oil paintings, implements of the Chinese, and collections of rifles, revolvers, and pocket watches. Downstairs is a four-cell jail and a doorway out to a backyard gallows.

Shasta's two cemeteries are worth seeking out. The closer, behind the courthouse along Trinity Alley, contains many stones from the 1850s. The tombstone for Hugh H. Burns, who died in 1853, reads: "Killed by Indians on Stillwater." To reach the second, an 1864 I.O.O.F. cemetery now maintained by the Masons, head east on State Route 299 toward Redding, turn right on Red

Right: *The 1855–56 Litsch Store and Bakery, located on the east end of Shasta, contains scores of new-old-stock items once sold there. Some of the canned goods are reproductions, but a park employee assured me that the champagne, wine, and liquor bottles were genuine and had never been opened. They were also inconveniently out of reach.*

Below: *The French Gulch Hotel and Dining Room has a bar that was fashioned in England, sent around Cape Horn to San Francisco, and carted overland to French Gulch.*

Bluff Road, go past the Shasta School, and turn right onto Mule Town Road. The cemetery will be on your left, a half mile from the main highway.

One more grave deserves your inspection. Less than a mile west of Shasta is a sign leading you to the grave site of Elchanan Broinshstein (Charles Brownstein), who died in 1864 at only seven months. His parents brought his body from Red Bluff to be buried in Shasta's Jewish Cemetery. The original headstone and forgotten cemetery were discovered in 1923 by highway engineers. The highway was rerouted to avoid the graveyard.

When You Go

Shasta is 5 miles west of Redding on State Route 299. (Note: Do not confuse this site with Mount Shasta, a town 60 miles north of Redding on Interstate 5, or Shasta Lake City, 7 miles north of Redding on Interstate 5.)

French Gulch

French miners exploring a gulch in 1849 or 1850 found significant gold deposits, and when a post office was granted in 1856, it honored its earliest pioneers and the location of their discovery: French Gulch.

From two water-driven stamp mills in 1851, the area grew in production to require eleven mills by 1900. The scurrying for gold grew to such a pace that in 1852 the Shasta *Courier* reported that in French Gulch "such rich diggings have been struck that miners are tearing down their houses to pursue the leads which run under them." Gold fever eventually cooled, but not before the mines produced almost $28 million in gold.

Walking and Driving Around French Gulch

The most attractive building in town today is the French Gulch Hotel and Dining Room, built in 1885 by Irishman Richard H. Feeney.

Across the street is the 1854 rock and mud Fox Store, which for most of its history was the E. Franck and Company Store. Up the street is a large, two-story 1906 I.O.O.F. Hall. North of the hall are several attractive, well-kept residences.

What was French Gulch's most photographed building, the lovely 1898 St. Rose's Catholic Church, was a charred ruin in 1999, the target of arsonists.

French Gulch features two cemeteries. The trail to the smaller Catholic cemetery, which begins on the southwest corner of French Gulch Road and Main Street, was posted against trespassing in 1999. Perhaps that was a necessary step, because when I visited in the early 1980s, I found a dozen monuments that had been systematically toppled.

To reach the public cemetery, drive north through town and turn west on Niagara Street. There you will find at least a dozen members of the Franck family, including F. A. and E. E., two of the founders of the E. Franck and Company Store. Incidentally, I did not find one obviously French name in either French Gulch cemetery.

French Gulch Road still winds past the remnants of several of the area's mines. The Milkmaid comes into view 2.4 miles from the intersection with Main Street. The large mill of the Washington Mine stands 1.1 miles beyond the Milkmaid.

When You Go

From Shasta, drive 9.7 miles west on State Route 299 to Trinity Mountain Road, the turnoff to French Gulch. French Gulch is 3 miles north.

Weaverville

Weaverville is more alive than any other site in this chapter. You will pass a great deal of modern America before you enter Weaverville's nineteenth-century historic district, but, once there, you will be charmed.

In 1850 George Weaver built a cabin at this spot, and within two years Weaverville had forty buildings and a population of 1,200. By 1854 the town had its first newspaper, and in 1858 a telegraph line linked the town to the outside world. Downtown Weaverville featured twenty-one brick buildings by 1859, nineteen of which still stand today.

Early Weaverville was fragmented into many ethnic sections, including a Chinatown. Most mining camps attempted to restrict mining by Chinese with ownership laws, excessive taxes, and officially or unofficially sanctioned violence. In Shasta, for example, the Chinese were summarily expelled in 1856. Weaverville was an exception. Although prejudice no doubt existed in the young camp, it was not town policy. As a result, Chinese began to settle there in great numbers, at one point constituting about half the population.

Walking and Driving Around Weaverville

By 1862 Weaverville had twenty-eight saloons, and one visitor complained that liquor, gambling, and fighting were the favorite pastimes of the citizenry. But Weaverville also had its sophisticated side as well, exemplified today by the stately buildings that remain in the central business district. A good example is the 1856 Trinity County Courthouse, at Court and Main streets. The building, constructed by Henry Hocker, originally served as a hotel, store, and saloon.

The most elegant and unusual structure in town is due to the Chinese. Because of their acceptance in the

Above, top: *To view the ornate interior of the Weaverville Joss House, you need to take an informative and inexpensive thirty-minute tour. The altar, sent from China, is reportedly more than 3,000 years old.*

Above, bottom: *The caretaker's quarters inside Won Lim Miao has a simple dining table and, at least by western standards, an even simpler bed.*

Won Lim Miao, "The Temple Amongst the Forest Beneath the Clouds," is part of a state historic park even as it continues to serve as an active temple.

Right: *The building currently housing Olson Stoneware is one of three two-story structures on Main Street demonstrating a Weaverville architectural curiosity: Each structure has an ornate spiral staircase leading from the sidewalk to the second floor. Although the buildings were two-story, the ownership of the two floors was separate, necessitating two independent entrances.*

Below: *This is the top floor of the three-story building constructed in Helena by Harm Schlomer in 1859. In 1861, the Schlomers lived in the top two floors and had a saloon in the basement. The building later became known as The Brewery, even though beer was actually brought from Weaverville. Over the years the building served as a schoolhouse, the site of an occasional Catholic Mass, and a combination office and residence.*

community, in 1853 they built a graceful Taoist temple. When that one burned, they built another in 1874 called Won Lim Miao, "The Temple Amongst the Forest Beneath the Clouds." The lovely building on Main Street is known to non-practitioners as the Weaverville Joss House.

Another worthwhile place to visit is the J. J. Jackson Memorial Museum, located east of the Joss House. The museum features era clothing, bottles, and apothecary paraphernalia, as well as samples of Native American crafts and ranching and mining memorabilia. In the basement are two cells from the 1880s that stood in the Trinity County Courthouse until 1968. Peer inside to see the interesting prisoners' graffiti and drawings adorning the walls.

Weaverville has two cemeteries. The larger is located on Oregon Street behind the Joss House. There you will find an unusually large number of elaborate antique stones among more modern ones. The oldest stone I found dated from 1859.

To visit the Catholic cemetery, return to Main Street. Go west to Court, turn right, and turn right again in two blocks at the Catholic church sign. This cemetery is adjacent to the lovely 1924 St. Patrick's Church, the fourth such building on the site. The previous three burned, but the present one closely resembles the others, the first of which dated from 1853. One prominent citizen buried there is Henry Hocker (1826–1882), builder of the courthouse.

At one time, Weaverville had three Chinese cemeteries, but no longer. The Chinese intended to return to China after making their fortune in America. Should they die in the United States before they returned to their homeland, the Chinese wanted their remains to be sent to China. The law, however, required their burial in California for sanitary reasons. The remains would have to stay buried for three years, but for a four-year period after that, the remains could be disinterred and shipped to China. After that four-year term expired, the remains were to be left undisturbed. For that reason, Chinese societies and organizations made certain that remains were properly disinterred and returned to China within that four-year period.

West of Weaverville is evidence of the mining that once enveloped the area. The La Grange Mine, 3.7 miles from town on State Route 299, was the world's largest hydraulic mine, with more than 100 million yards of gravel hosed down from the hillside to release about $3.5 million in gold. A hydraulic monitor, a kind of water cannon, stands next to the highway. You can see, across the canyon and in the fragile vegetation behind you, the environmental devastation the process caused.

When You Go
Weaverville is 44 miles northwest of Redding and 28.5 miles northwest of the turnoff to French Gulch on State Route 299.

Helena
Helena was a delightful surprise for me. On my first visit, the afternoon light gave Helena's brick buildings a warm look, and absolutely no one was there to disturb the serenity of the spot. The town features about a dozen buildings under roof, most sheltered by drooping trees or partially obscured by shrubs.

The first mining camp in the area was lightheartedly called Bagdad because of its exotic and international nature: *Trinity County Historic Sites* reports that "ladies of accommodation" who settled there came from various countries. A Bagdad miner described them as "mademoiselles, señoritas, and jungfraus." Bagdad was on the east side of the North Fork of the Trinity River. On the west side another camp grew, known simply as North Fork.

John Meckel and his younger brother Christian came to North Fork in 1853 and opened a general merchandise store and pack train business. Two years later Harmon Schlomer arrived and opened a blacksmith shop and eventually built a toll bridge and a three-story brick building. The history of North Fork essentially became the history of the Meckel and Schlomer families. Their stories became intertwined when John Meckel and Harm Schlomer married sisters.

In 1870, Christian Meckel went to Germany and returned with a bride, Helena. In 1891, the town's post office name was changed in her honor and to avoid confusion with another North Fork in California. By then, the men of Helena were only part-time miners, with most augmenting their incomes as farmers. Helena, with its orchards, grape arbors, and clear rivers, became a favorite Sunday-outing destination for young men and women from Weaverville.

As you enter Helena today, the first building you will notice is a moody, red brick, three-story edifice, known as The Brewery, erected by Harm Schlomer in 1859.

Up the road is the wooden Schlomer Clubhouse and Sleeping Quarters. Across the street stands another sturdy brick building, the 1858 Meckel Brothers General Merchandise, which also housed the post office. The Brewery and the Meckel Brothers Store are the only two surviving historic brick structures in Trinity County not in Weaverville.

Across the street to the west is Harm Schlomer's wooden feed store and stable.

The Callahan Ranch Hotel closed in the 1930s. The scaffolding along the north side has been there since at least the early 1980s, when I first visited Callahan.

The Helena Cemetery stands southeast of town. Return to State Route 299, cross the bridge going east and stop to read the historical marker about Bagdad. Immediately beyond that marker, turn left from the highway. That road takes you in a few yards to what is now called the Trinity County Cemetery.

There are ten marked graves of the pioneer Schlomer family, including H. [Harmon] K. Schlomer (1825–1898).

Most of the Meckel family members left Helena and returned to Weaverville, where several are buried in both the public and Catholic cemeteries. Only Edna Meckel (1883–1946) has a marker in the Helena Cemetery.

When You Go
From Weaverville, drive 14.2 miles west on State Route 299. Turn right on East Fork Road and proceed .3 of a mile to Helena.

Callahan

Callahan, located at the south end of Scott Valley at the junctions of the east and south forks of the Scott River, was named for M. B. Callahan, who built the first cabin in 1851 and opened a hotel the following year. He sold the hotel and left the area in 1855, but by 1857 the Callahan Ranch Hotel was serving as a stage station— the first in Siskiyou County—for the California and Oregon Stage Company, whose stages traversed a toll road from Shasta through Callahan and on to Yreka. When the post office opened in 1858, it was for Callahans Ranch, a name shortened to Callahan in 1892. The stage route became obsolete in 1887 when the Central Pacific Railroad was completed between San Francisco and Portland. The gold deposits that first brought people to the valley played out in the 1890s, although dredging operations continued into the 1950s. Dredging evidence extends for several miles north of Callahan.

The Caldwell Store, sitting in perpetual shade on the south side of the street in Hamburg, has lost its front porch and its westernmost section.

Walking and Driving Around Callahan

If you are coming from Weaverville, on your right as you enter Callahan is the town's most photogenic building, the wood-frame, two-story 1854 Callahan Ranch Hotel.

Across the street are three connected commercial buildings. On the south end is Callahan's only active business at this writing, the Callahan Emporium, which opened in the early days of the twentieth century. In the middle is the 1890, two-story, cut-stone A. H. Denny Building. Next to it is the Mount of Bolivar Grange (Mount Bolivar is south of Callahan).

Next door to the Callahan Ranch Hotel stands the two-story Farringtons Hotel, which operated from 1867 until 1925. When I visited in the 1980s and mid-1990s, part of the building was open to sell groceries and gasoline, with the Farrington family still running the business. When I returned in 1999, a sign on the door an-

nounced, "After 130 years of continued service to the community of Callahan, the Farrington family is no longer in business. . . . Thank you for your business and your friendship through the years."

To visit Callahan's cemeteries, turn west immediately south of the Emporium. South Fork Road takes you past the 1894 community church, originally the Congregational church. Land for the church was donated by A. H. Denny in memory of his wife, Elisa, who had hoped the town would someday have a Protestant church. The building has an unusual, attractive, wave pattern in its shingled siding.

Beyond the community church is a large boulder on the left side of the road with a plaque that denotes the site of Scott Valley's first Catholic church, erected in about 1858. Just beyond that marker is Callahan's Protestant Cemetery. There you will see headstones for several members of the Denny family, including Elisa Webber Denny, who died in 1881 at thirty-nine. Several markers remind us that the name of the town has changed slightly: Headstones have the town as "Callahans," "Callahan's," and "Callahan."

A short distance south is the Catholic Cemetery, which has a poignant double marker for James and Fidelia Littlefield, both of whom died, at ages eight and six, respectively, on December 15, 1877. One can almost hear their parents' grief with the epitaph: "Our Children— Rest Beloved Ones Rest."

When You Go
Callahan is 61 miles north of Weaverville on State Route 3.

Hamburg

Hamburg, originally known as Hamburg Bar, was founded and named in the early 1850s by Sigmond Simon, probably for the German seaport. The camp was the site of significant placer gold strikes between 1856 and 1859. But the placer gold was exhausted by 1863, the same year that a Klamath River flood washed away most of the town. Hamburg then had little gold and few build-ings, but it was not dead yet. The rebuilt town eventually survived as a trading center for area mines and even received the official stamp of legitimacy—a post office— in 1878.

Today a few vacant buildings, clearly posted against trespassers, stand on either side of the highway through Hamburg. If you are coming from the east, slow down when you see Sarah Totten Campground. In that campground are piles of stones lifted from the Klamath in the 1850s by miners searching for placer gold in the sand beneath. According to an interpretive sign, those miners had some success, finding nuggets of up to sixteen ounces.

Hamburg begins west of the campground. Several older residences, some occupied, stand on either side of the road, followed by the old Caldwell Store on the highway's south side .7 of a mile west of the campground turnoff. The wood frame structure was built by Dan Caldwell and operated until the 1930s, when it was closed by its last owner, Caldwell's sister-in-law, Sarah Totten, for whom the campground is named.

A stout stone wall stands beyond the Caldwell Store before the highway crosses Mack Creek. Immediately

The old Hamburg Schoolhouse, now a private residence, stands partially hidden from view across the street from the entrance to the cemetery.

beyond the creek crossing is a turnoff to the left that heads a few yards to the Hamburg Cemetery. The 1867 graveyard, almost invisible from the road, is one of the more picturesque in this chapter. It sits on a stony hillside, so it is difficult to determine how many are buried there, but one has the feeling that there are far more graves than markers. One of the largest markers is for storekeeper Dan Caldwell (1838–1896), who is now "Sheltered and Safe from Sorrow."

A modern Hamburg shows signs of life still farther west along State Route 96.

When You Go

Hamburg is 53 miles northwest of Callahan and 41 miles northwest of Yreka. From Callahan, drive north on State Route 3 for 18.5 miles to Quartz Valley Road. Turn left and proceed 9.4 miles, where it intersects with Scott River Road. Turn left and go 20 miles to the tiny settlement of Scott Bar (and its attractive community hall, formerly a school). Beyond Scott Bar 3.1 miles, turn left on State Route 96. Hamburg is 1.8 miles west of that junction. Both Quartz Valley and Scott River roads are paved but often narrow.

Ingot

Ingot is not a destination ghost town, but you will pass through it as you head toward the best site in northeastern California, Fort Bidwell.

The first remnant of interest, .4 of a mile before you get to Ingot as you come from Redding, stands across Little Cow Creek east of the highway: a smelter foundation on a small rise at a spot noted as Tollgate on the old Millville 15' topographic map.

Ingot itself is a series of small buildings strung along the west side of the highway beyond the foundation.

A second, more impressive, site stands a half mile beyond Ingot, also on the right side of the highway. There you will find the remnants of the Coronado Mine workings: an ore sorter, a mill, and a machine shop. All are perched on a hillside eroding into Little Cow Creek.

Ingot was named for a foundry that cast ore from the nearby smelter into ingots between 1905 and 1909. There were not many ingots, however. The prophetically named Afterthought Mining Company invested well over a million dollars in the early 1920s before abandoning its holdings, and the California Zinc Company failed in its

A machine shop (left) and the remains of a mill (right) of the Coronado Mine stand above Little Cow Creek just beyond Ingot.

efforts to process zinc and copper a few years later. The town had a post office from 1919 until 1940.

When You Go

Ingot is 18 miles northeast of Redding on State Route 299.

Fort Bidwell and High Grade

Fort Bidwell is the northeastern-most town in California. That geographical curiosity is the least reason to visit it. The best is that Fort Bidwell is one of California's most appealing out-of-the-way spots.

Nearby, on a wonderfully scenic road, are the sparse remains of High Grade.

Fort Bidwell

As you enter somnolent Fort Bidwell, you will notice several unoccupied residential and commercial buildings among the occupied. The first building of note, on the east side of the road, is the community church, which has served the town since 1885.

The most photogenic building, farther up the street on the west side, is Kober's Dry Goods Store, probably built in the late 1880s; it is closed at this writing. On the south outside wall of Kober's, partially hidden by trees and bushes, is an old Levi's sign featuring the promise "A New Pair Free If They Rip." Nearby is a large vault, the only remains of the 1907 Bank of Fort Bidwell, which failed during the Depression. A gray cut-stone two-story building, it was demolished for its fine stone, which was shipped elsewhere. Some said that the proceeds from the sale of the stone would help pay off those who lost their savings, but longtime resident Pat Barry laments, "I certainly never saw a penny of it."

Other interesting buildings along Main Street north of Kober's include a brick commercial building and the Fort Bidwell Hotel.

To reach a particularly well-kept cemetery, follow North Street as it heads west from Main Street. From the cemetery you have a sweeping view of the town itself, Surprise Valley, Upper Alkali Lake, and, behind you, the Warner Mountains.

In the graveyard are both civilian and military headstones. Among the civilians are store owner Henry Kober (1871–1961) and his wife Caroline (1878–1948). Among the military is a stone for Sgt. Frank Lewis, which reads in part: "This monument was erected by his company comrades as a testimonial of their love for one who was a universal favorite with all who knew him." He died in 1877 at age thirty.

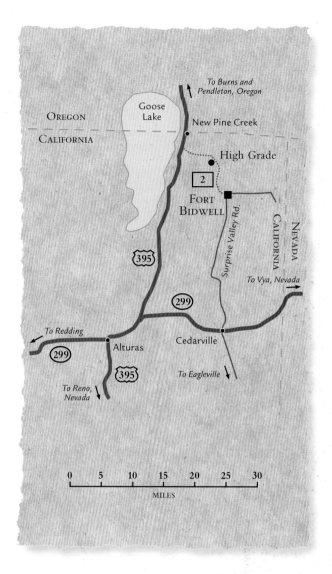

At the north end of Main Street stands what appears to be a sturdy school. I say "appears" because it was closed in 1956 as not earthquake safe.

There is much more to see in Fort Bidwell. Return south on Main to Bridge Street, where a sign directs you west to the 1876 stone block Fort Bidwell General Store. Two attractive residences stand nearby.

West of the store are the remains of old Fort Bidwell. A cavalry post from 1865 to 1892, the fort was named for John Bidwell, an early California frontiersman, general in the California militia, congressman, and presidential candidate on the 1892 Prohibition ticket. For all the things that he did, however, one thing he did not do was visit the fort named in his honor.

Fort Bidwell became an Indian boarding school after it was decommissioned. The property was largely dismantled in the 1930s as a WPA project, but several buildings remain on what is now the center of the Northern

On the northwest corner of the Fort Bidwell parade grounds stands the decaying old schoolhouse, formerly a chapel.

Kober's Dry Goods Store features an old Levi's sign with the promise "A New Pair Free If They Rip." Below that vow is the old Levi's logo of two horses attempting to go opposite directions. They are prevented by the single pair of jeans attached to each.

Paiute Fort Bidwell Indian Reservation. On the left as you approach the old parade grounds is a large, abandoned, reservation boarding house, and on a western hill are the stone ruins of the hospital. Beyond the northwest corner of the parade grounds stands the Fort Bidwell Chapel, which later served as a school.

When You Go
Fort Bidwell is 26 miles north of Cedarville on Surprise Valley Road and 191 miles northeast of Redding. (Note: Explore Cedarville before heading to Fort Bidwell. Cedarville features some architecturally interesting businesses, a Masonic Lodge, the United Church of Christ, and several attractive older residences.)

High Grade
Take the drive northwest from Fort Bidwell for the absolutely lovely scenery, not for the scant ruins of the High Grade Mining District. You climb out of Fort Bidwell into the Warner Mountains on a dirt road that is steep and occasionally rutted but nevertheless suited for a two-wheel-drive truck. The road rises to about 7,600 feet elevation (about 3,000 feet above Fort Bidwell), crests, and drops to New Pine Creek, which straddles the Cali-fornia-Oregon border along the edge of Goose Lake.

The High Grade District was mined from 1905, when a teenage sheepherder discovered gold, until 1918. Although the town of High Grade had a post office, a restaurant, a bar, and hotels, the district hardly warranted a strike-it-rich stampede. During High Grade's thirteen years, less than $100,000 in gold was actually extracted. Since then, the area has seen only sporadic activity, although some claims were still being worked in the 1990s.

The best of the scant ruins of the High Grade District come at 9.1 miles from the turnoff at Fort Bidwell, where the road makes a hairpin turn. There you will find remnants of the Klondyke Group—a toppled mill, with several iron boilers, and a leaning log cabin.

Beyond the Klondyke a half mile is a turnoff to one of my favorite place names in California—Dismal Swamp. Two-tenths of a mile beyond that turnoff is the Lodgepole Mining Claim, where a roofless log cabin stands.

When You Go
From Fort Bidwell, head northwest on County Road 2, which begins near the old school's entrance north of town. The road goes for 17 miles to New Pine Creek.

High Grade's Klondyke Mill, like most others, was built on a hillside to utilize gravity. Now gravity is getting the last laugh.

Chapter Four

GHOSTS OF SAN FRANCISCO BAY

Main photo: *Ruins of the warden's house on Alcatraz provide an unusual framing of San Francisco and the Transamerica Pyramid, while two seagulls steal the scene.*

Inset photo: *China Camp is reflected in the window of a fisherman's cabin.*

Ghost town enthusiasts usually visit the sights of the San Francisco Bay area as a separate activity from ghost towning. But you may be surprised to know that seven ghosts are located close to San Francisco, and one more sits isolated in the hills to the south.

Unlike the rest of this book, not one site in this chapter was a gold camp. The premier attraction is Alcatraz, a great ghost prison, but a ghost town as well. Angel Island offers two ghost forts. China Camp is a ghost fishing village and a reminder that injustices done to the Chinese were not confined to the Mother Lode. Somersville recalls that not all mines are for precious metals. Locke is a unique Chinese agricultural settlement. New Almaden and New Idria, named for counterparts in Spain and Austria, featured a mineral rare in the world and essential in the recovery of gold. And there is Drawbridge, perhaps the most unusual site in this book: a duck-hunters' ghost town.

Alcatraz

Alcatraz was "a small town with a big jail," according to former head guard Philip Bergen. In addition to its "big jail," Alcatraz was home to about 300 civilians who shopped in the small store, received mail at the post office, and attended events in a social hall that featured a bowling alley. Among those civilians were sixty to eighty children who played on a cement playground (no cap pistols or rubber knives, however) and were ferried daily to school in San Francisco, a mere one-and-a-quarter miles away. Bergen's daughter remembers fondly, "It was a great place to grow up. . . . There were parties for kids, formal dances for the teens. We were within steps of the prison, but no one locked their doors."

Those children and their parents have gone, and Alcatraz is now a small *ghost* town with a big *ghost* jail. It is also one of the West's most fascinating places to visit.

Isla de Alcatraces (Spanish for "Pelican Island") was the name bestowed in 1775 on what is now known as Yerba Buena Island in San Francisco Bay. The name was transferred to the place now popularly called "The Rock" in 1826.

The Gold Rush made Alcatraz important. The amazing Mother Lode brought hundreds of ships with tens of thousands of people to San Francisco

From 1934 until 1963, convicts arriving at Alcatraz knew that this was the end of the prison line.

through the Golden Gate, and Alcatraz had the Pacific Coast's first lighthouse, built in 1854, to usher them in safely. When the Civil War broke out, San Francisco's enormous gold supply tempted the Confederacy, but by that time Alcatraz also was the Pacific Coast's first permanent military outpost, with 111 cannons and rows of gun emplacements. The strength of Alcatraz and other fortifications deterred the Confederacy, and not one shot was fired from the battlements. (That might have been fortunate, because during an 1876 centennial celebration, a ship was towed into range for Alcatraz's mighty cannons to obliterate. They failed.)

In addition to its navigational and strategic importance, Alcatraz has a long history as a prison. As early as 1859, it was an army disciplinary barracks. During the Civil War, it housed deserters and other military miscreants along with citizens accused of treason and the crew of a Confederate privateer. In the late 1800s, it held prisoners from various Indian wars, including members of the Modoc, Apache, and Hopi tribes. After the 1906 San Francisco earthquake, the island housed 106 of the city's inmates, as its jail was in ruins.

In 1907, Alcatraz was deemed no longer necessary for defense, and it was converted to a full-time military prison. Construction began in 1908 on the huge cell house that still dominates the island, a structure that was at the time the world's largest steel-reinforced concrete building. It was designed so cells had neither an outside wall nor an outside ceiling—escaping one's cell would still leave the inmate within the building's walls. The prisoners who

Miners in the coal mines of Somersville and the quicksilver mines of New Almaden and New Idria needed lamps like the Carbide Justrite Victor Cap Lamp to light their way through their mines' miles of tunnels.

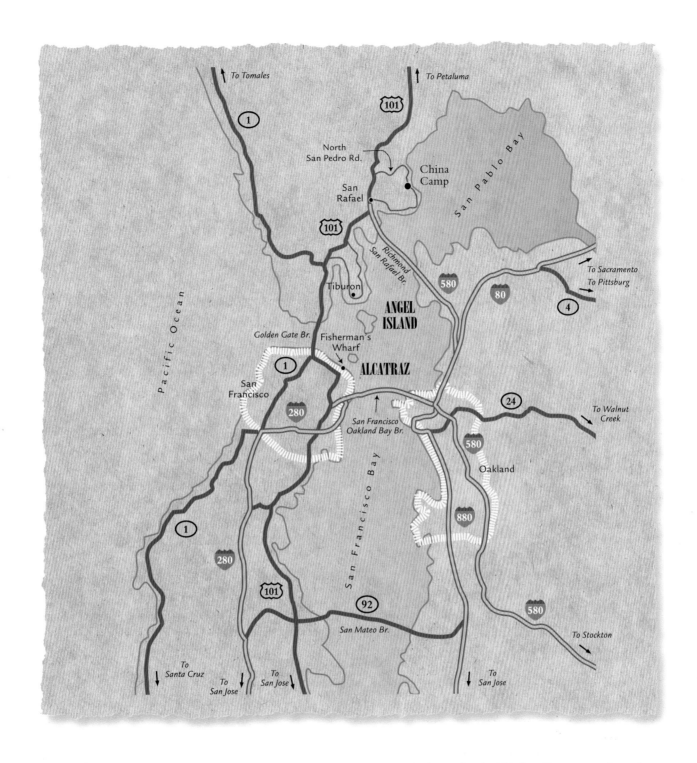

helped construct the cell house were its first occupants when it was completed in 1912.

The federal penitentiary that gave the island its notoriety was opened in 1934 as a place to house inmates whose behavior at other federal prisons made them particular risks. Here, on a chilly, desolate battleship of land, inmates were scrutinized by one staff member for every three prisoners (as opposed to the normal federal ratio of one to ten) and counted as many as fourteen times daily. Among the most infamous were Al Capone, "Machine Gun" Kelly, and Robert Stroud, the "Bird Man of Alcatraz," who in fact had birds at Leavenworth penitentiary, not at Alcatraz.

The food was good and prisoners were not mistreated physically, despite Hollywood's various depictions. But there was one cruel punishment: the proximity of the lights and sounds of San Francisco. As one inmate reported, "There was never a day when you couldn't see what you were losing." On New Year's Eve, it was said that inmates could even hear champagne corks popping at shoreline clubs.

The average stay at Alcatraz was from eight to ten

Left: *Various wildflowers and untended roses bloom within the warden's house. The fireplace's tiles give a hint of the former glory of the residence, which was built in the 1920s for the commander of the military prison.*

Below: *The Post Exchange and Officers' Club (left), which dates from 1910, burned in June 1970. During the years of the prison, the Officers' Club featured a gymnasium, dance floor, bowling alley, and soda fountain. Behind it is the island's power plant.*

Facing page: *Alcatraz's warden lived in a large, seventeen-room home in the Mission-Revival style. It was one of several buildings that burned in June 1970 during the Native American occupation of the island.*

years; the longest was three months short of twenty-eight years, which was virtually the length of time the prison was in service. It closed in 1963 because buildings were deteriorating and the prison was overly expensive to run. Of the 1,545 men who did time over those twenty-nine years, eight were murdered, five committed suicide, seven were killed attempting to escape, and two were eventually executed at San Quentin for killing two Alcatraz guards. No successful escape is known, although five inmates were presumed drowned in San Francisco Bay. One inmate in 1962 actually made it to rocks near Golden Gate Bridge, but he was too exhausted to climb to dry land and was apprehended.

After Alcatraz's closing in 1963, the island was uninhabited, except for a caretaker, until November 1969, when fourteen Native American students invaded the island. Eventually a group calling itself the "Indians of All Tribes" claimed possession of Alcatraz under a Sioux treaty of 1868 guaranteeing that abandoned federal lands would revert to Indians. The occupiers sardonically claimed that the island would be an ideal place for Indians since it was isolated from modern facilities, had inadequate sanitation, no running water, high unemployment, and no educational facilities. It was also a place where the population had always been held as prisoners and kept dependent upon others. The federal authorities were not amused and eventually cut off electricity and water supplies before evicting the Indians in June 1971.

Scars of that occupation remain on Alcatraz. A fire on June 2, 1970, destroyed the lighthouse keeper's home, the once-lovely warden's residence, and the post exchange.

Walking Around Alcatraz

I suggest, when you arrive at Alcatraz, to try to forget the prison's cinematic portrayals and see it for what it was, because former inmate Jim Quillan worries that movies, books, and legends have glorified the prison. He reminds us that Alcatraz was "about isolation, sadness, anger, and death." Glenn Williams, another inmate, says simply: "This was a horrible, horrible place."

Understanding Alcatraz's reality is much easier if you take the tape-recorded tour of the cell house. It is narrated by former guards and inmates and features the sounds of clanging doors and the echoes of men's voices. The effect is mesmerizing.

Built by the army in the 1920s on top of the guardhouse and sally port, this building has always been known as "The Chapel," although there is no record of its ever being used for that purpose. Its principal function during both military and prison duty was as a quarters for single men.

Wildflowers extend down a ramp, providing a cheerfulness that was noticeably lacking during the island's prison days. The buildings in the background are, from left, a storehouse; the post exchange/officers' club; and the 1857 guardhouse and sally port, which is the island's oldest building.

114

During the years of the federal penitentiary, many corrections officers and their families walked through the doors of their apartment building, which had been erected as a military barracks in 1905.

Inside their apartment building, families of corrections officers on Alcatraz could patronize this tiny market and its post office.

After the tape tour, be sure to walk everywhere you are permitted to go. Purchase one of the various brochures and maps and make a thorough exploration of corridors and walking paths. Be certain to visit to the recreation yard. From there you can see the inmates' views of the Bay Area, so close but yet so distant.

Much of the ghost prison remains, but little of the ghost town. On the island's southeast end, you can look down to a large parade ground (on my last visit, hundreds of seagulls were in formation) that served as the playground for the town's children. Adjacent to that space are the considerable ruins of the apartments, bulldozed in 1971, that their families lived in. Families also lived in the former military barracks, the four-story building standing adjacent to the wharf where your ferry docked.

When You Go

Ferries leave San Francisco's Fisherman's Wharf to Alcatraz Island on a frequent basis, but advance reservations are essential. Incidentally, neither food nor drink is sold on the island.

Angel Island

Angel Island offers one of the premier day trips of the Bay Area. Visitors leave behind the human tumult and San Francisco's exorbitantly priced real estate to discover solitude, relaxation, and, yes, even ghost towns—or at least ghost forts.

Isla de Los Angeles was named in 1775 by Lt. Juan Manuel de Ayala, commander of the packet *San Carlos*, which anchored in the cove that now bears Ayala's name. Angel Island has been the site of Indian villages, a Spanish rancho, a hangout for thieves and a dueling ground, a Civil War fortification, a sandstone quarry, a military detention center, a quarantine station, an army base, an immigration facility, and even a Nike missile base. Remains of several of these deployments stand on the island today, creating a day-long adventure for naturalists, photographers, and ghost town enthusiasts.

Hiking, Cycling, or Riding the Tram on Angel Island

You will dock at Ayala Cove, which, beginning in 1891, housed a quarantine station where foreign ships were fumigated and possibly contagious immigrants were isolated. A two-story attendants' quarters from that era now houses a museum.

A tram that circumnavigates the island leaves from Ayala Cove. If, however, you want more than a cursory glance at the highlights of the island, I cannot recommend it. It stops for only a few minutes at the island's three major attractions, which would be very frustrating for a photographer, for example. The tram driver will let

you off at the attractions, but you can only board a later tram on a space-available basis, a chancy proposition. In addition, at this writing the tram features a radio-wave-generated audio that is occasionally indecipherable due to static.

If you really desire to investigate Angel Island, I recommend walking or, as I did on another visit, riding a mountain bicycle. I spent more than four hours on the island (you are limited somewhat by ferry schedules) and rode almost ten miles. You can bring your own bike on the ferry or rent one on the island.

Southwest of Ayala Cove is Camp Reynolds, established in 1863 to repel a possible Confederate attack on San Francisco and its enormous gold supply. More than a dozen buildings stand near a parade ground sloping toward the bay. Near the shore stands a large brick warehouse built in 1909 that housed camp supplies and ordnance for the island's gun emplacements.

On the southeast end of Angel Island are the considerable remains of Fort McDowell. Begun in 1899 as a detainment facility for soldiers returning from the Spanish-American War who had been exposed to contagious diseases, the facility became known as Fort McDowell two years later when it became a discharge center for the same war. In 1910, Fort McDowell was greatly enlarged and became a military induction center. During World War II, the fort was a crucial point of embarkation for troops bound for the Pacific.

Most of Fort McDowell's buildings date from the 1910 enlargement. You will enter along Officers' Row, a stately procession of two-story, red-tiled residences, some of which house park employees. The major structures of Fort McDowell are down the road: a chapel, a combination mess hall and gymnasium, a supply store, artillery headquarters, an administration building, and a hulking 600-man barracks.

On the north side of Angel Island is an immigration station that began operation in 1905. Unlike New York's Ellis Island, this facility was not built to welcome and process immigrants but rather to attempt to exclude them, as most arriving at the station were Chinese during a period of anti-Asian sentiment. Only Chinese who could prove they had relatives in this country could enter, a process made trickier when the 1906 earthquake and subsequent fire destroyed immigration records. Founda-

Camp Reynolds's officers' quarters—boarded-up, grayish-white, two-story wooden residences—appear to be standing at frozen attention beside the parade ground.

Above: *Ghost town enthusiasts are accustomed to the partial remnants of buildings that were flimsy when built and meant to last only for a bonanza's duration. Fort McDowell is different. It looks as if it could withstand anything on the Richter Scale that San Francisco could take.*

Left: *Although the buildings themselves seem to be holding up rather well on Fort McDowell's Officers' Row, the same cannot be said for some of the steps, railings, and porches.*

Inside the immigration station on the north side of Angel Island is a re-creation of the crowded quarters that Asians endured while waiting to join relatives in the United States.

Many Chinese, bitter about the long delays in getting processed through immigration, wrote poetry on the walls of their "prison." A booklet available at the immigration center offers translations of their despair and frustration.

tions of a hospital, five standing buildings (many obscured by foliage), and a barracks make up the site, along with a marker in memory of the 175,000 Chinese who were detained here. The station closed in 1940.

When You Go
Visit Angel Island by ferry from San Francisco or Tiburon, or by private boat. Ferry reservations are highly recommended.

China Camp

China Camp, a small fishing village that is now part of a beautiful state park on the shores of San Pablo Bay, tells an important story about the Chinese in the San Francisco area.

In 1879, John McNear leased twelve acres of bay shore land to Richard Bullis, who in turn sublet the land to Chinese shrimp fishermen. The settlement that became known as China Camp was one of five fishing villages that grew around Point San Pedro, north of San Rafael. Because maritime regulations decreed that only white men could be captains of ships forty feet or longer, Bullis made weekly voyages to circumvent the law for his Chinese lessees, who eventually made up a camp of 469 people, all adult males except fifty. The camp featured a school, a barber shop, three mercantiles, and a marine supply store.

Within five years, the shrimping operation was extremely successful, with the fishermen using efficient bag nets that utilized the actions of the tides. Between 1885 and 1892, the average annual catch for the entire bay was 5.4 million pounds of shrimp, most of it dried and exported to China. China Camp was one of the leading producers of bay shrimp.

Shrimping became an important California industry, but the Chinese fishermen were attacked on two fronts: by white fishermen who resented their hard-working rivals and by conservationists who feared that the bay was being severely over-fished.

In 1901, the California legislature passed a law banning fishing during the height of the season and in 1905 passed another prohibiting the exportation of shrimp, effectively crippling the industry.

In the following year, two disasters hit Bay Area Chinese. The first was a suspicious fire that destroyed Pacific Grove's Chinese section, and the second was the great earthquake and fire that destroyed San Francisco. As a result, many Chinese found refuge in a tent city at China Camp, a place largely out of business but, because of its isolation, free from persecution. By 1911, laws were passed prohibiting the use of bag nets and making the possession of dried shrimp unlawful. The industry was moribund for four years and would never fully recover.

In 1915, some restrictions were eased, and China Camp came back to limited life into the 1930s, but eventually only one company remained, operated by the Quan family, who were the last Chinese fishermen on San Pablo Bay. The remains of their company stand at China Camp today.

Those remains consist of almost a dozen buildings. A visitors' center located in a shrimp-drying shed displays

Above: *The shrimp-drying shed at China Camp contains items common to the town's fishermen along with a history of the area and historical photographs.*

Left: *From this pier in San Pablo Bay the China Camp fishermen launched the most successful shrimping operation in northern California—so successful that the California legislature passed laws restricting their trade.*

memorabilia and photographs. Nearby stands a long brick heater covered by a wooden roof where shrimp were dried using blowing fans. The remainder of China Camp consists of a pier, residences, a Flying A gasoline pump (featuring fuel at 49.9¢ per gallon), and a small cafe. The cafe formerly offered Tacoma beer ("Best From East to West"), cooked crab, and shrimp cocktail. You can still purchase the latter when the cafe is open on weekends.

When You Go

China Camp is north of San Rafael. Exit U.S. 101 on North San Pedro Road and go east for 4.7 miles. There you will find the park office, which has a helpful brochure and map. The village is .4 of a mile beyond the park office.

Somersville
(The Black Diamond Mines)

Somersville and its four vanished neighbors—Nortonville, Stewartville, West Hartley, and Judsonville—made up the Mount Diablo Coal Field, which between 1860 and 1914 produced almost four million tons of coal in the state's largest coal-mining district. Although not as precious as gold, silver, or copper, coal nevertheless can be a "black diamond" when found in substantial quantities.

The town was named for Francis Somers, who in 1859 was one of the discoverers of the Black Diamond vein. The town grew to a population of about 1,000 and featured wooden homes and businesses on practically treeless, grassy, rolling hills. That is a natural combination for fire, and Nortonville, Somersville's larger neighbor to the west, had its business district destroyed in 1878.

In 1885, the Black Diamond Company ceased operations when superior coal deposits were found in Washington. The company took some fortunate Mount Diablo miners with them. Of the ones left behind, the Contra Costa *Gazette* declared sadly, "The few inhabitants still remaining are hopelessly stranded, with no possibility of relief."

Although some coal mining continued until the beginning of World War I, the best days were over. Dozens of buildings from Somersville and its sister coal towns were dismantled for salvage or moved to nearby communities and ranches. The last mining in the area, from the 1920s until 1949, was for a commodity even less precious than coal—silica-laden sand for a glass company in Oakland and a steel foundry in nearby Pittsburg.

Walking Around Somersville

The coal towns are gone, but the Black Diamond Mines Regional Preserve, a hiking and picnicking area, remains to protect the remnants of Mount Diablo's mining history.

As you pass the park entrance, on your left stand six buildings, four of which formerly stood at Somersville. The town itself was located near the park's parking lot, almost a mile south.

The park's visitors' center is located a quarter of a mile beyond the parking area in the Greathouse Portal, one of the tunnels of the Hazel Atlas sand mining operation. Memorabilia, photographs, and a video provide a closer look at the now-vanished coal communities. You can also make reservations for an hour-long tour of the Hazel Atlas Mine.

On a hill west of the Somersville site is the Rose Hill Cemetery, the best—but bittersweet—reason to visit the Black Diamond preserve. The cemetery, which is a ten- to fifteen-minute hike from the picnic area, has many interesting and touching headstones and an excellent panorama of the Somersville site. Many nationalities are represented in the cemetery with a preponderance of Welsh. As you might expect, several buried here died in mine accidents.

Those who explore old cemeteries are accustomed to seeing a large number of children's graves, but this graveyard has a disturbing percentage of headstones for the young, many of whom died of diphtheria, typhoid, and scarlet fever. Four children of the Jenkins family, for example, died within seven years of each other, none reaching the age of nine. Three children of David and Lizzie Bowman are buried here; none lived to the age of two. The epitaph of Julia Etta, who died in 1870 at two years of age, could apply for all the children: "Too sweet a flower to bloom on earth, she has gone to bloom in heaven."

When You Go

Somersville is southeast of Pittsburg and southwest of Antioch. On State Route 4 between the two towns, take the Somersville Road South exit. Take Somersville Road south for 2.8 miles, following signs to the Black Diamond Mines Regional Preserve.

Locke

Locke is a town of unique history and considerable architectural charm. It came into being in 1916 when a group of Chinese leased land from George, Clay, and Lloyd Locke to construct residences and businesses after nearby Walnut Grove's Chinatown had burned the previous year. The Chinese could only lease land because California's Alien Land Act, passed in 1913, prohibited Asians from owning land. (Incredibly, that law was not repealed until deemed unconstitutional in 1952.)

The community known as Locke (pronounced by non-English-speaking Chinese as "Lockee") was built in less than a year using Chinese capital but white carpen-

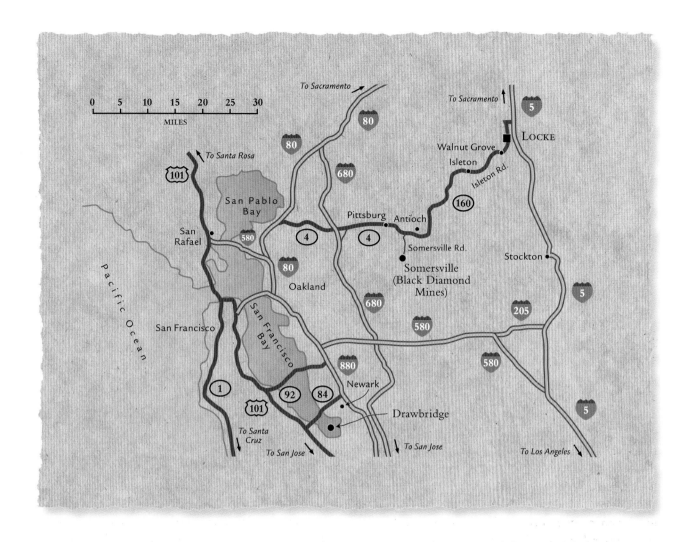

ters. With a resident population of about 600 and about 1,000 more during various crop-growing seasons, Locke contained every imaginable legitimate business—grocery stores, shoe repair shops, slaughterhouses, canneries, and gambling halls. The gambling halls were considered quite respectable, as they also served as social centers and a place to secure laborers. But there were many illegitimate enterprises as well: Opium dens, brothels (run and staffed by whites), and speakeasies during Prohibition flourished in hidden back rooms and second stories of otherwise legal enterprises. Locke had no official law enforcement.

The citizens of Locke were primarily agricultural workers who traveled among neighboring farms harvesting a variety of crops, with asparagus and Bartlett pears prominent among them.

Most of the town's remaining Chinese residents today have lived long lives in Locke, but the younger generation largely has left for more lucrative opportunities elsewhere.

Walking Around Locke

When you arrive in Locke, you will see, across from a large warehouse, a row of wooden buildings on the east side of the street. These are unusual because, as they face west, they are actually the second stories of structures whose first stories face east on Main Street, the next street over. For example, the seventh building from the south once served as a theater for traveling Chinese repertory companies. Its first floor, facing east on Main, was a gambling hall.

Go north to Locke Street, turn right, and park in the nearby lot. Then take a stroll along a street unique in the West, featuring fragile wood structures with overhanging second-story balconies.

The first building of note, the single-story Joe Shoong School, is on the northwest corner of Locke and Main. The 1926 school was funded by and named for the millionaire founder of the National Dollar stores.

The other buildings on the west side of the street are the ones whose second stories you saw one block west.

123

Locke is unique in the United States because it is the country's last rural Chinese town. It was placed on the National Register of Historic Places in 1971.

The series of wood-frame structures that face west along the road passing Locke are the second stories of the principal commercial buildings of Locke's Main Street.

Students did not attend Locke's Joe Shoong School for their regular studies; they would attend classes there after returning home from a segregated Asian elementary school in Walnut Grove. At the Joe Shoong School they learned about Chinese art, culture, and language.

The business that is likely to be the center of activity when you visit, especially if it is a weekend, stands in the middle of Main Street's east side. It is Al's Place, built in 1916 as Lee Bing's Restaurant. It was purchased by Al Adami in 1941 and has been known by the gloriously politically incorrect name of "Al the Wop's" ever since. Have you ever slathered peanut butter on a steak? It is *de rigueur* at Al's (and delicious).

Locke's most fascinating building is the Dai Loy ("Big Welcome") Gambling Hall, home of Locke's museum.

The museum sells a booklet, "Discovering Locke," which has a helpful map for exploring the town, along with a brief history of the town. For more information, consider purchasing *Bitter Melon*, which contains interviews with Locke residents. From that volume comes a simple, telling reason to explore this picturesque town: "Locke is the most visible monument to the extraordinary efforts made by the Chinese to develop agriculture in California and establish communities in rural America."

When You Go

Locke is 35.5 miles northeast of Somersville. From the Black Diamond Regional Preserve, return to State Route 4 and go east. The freeway will turn north and cross the San Joaquin River, becoming State Route 160. Stay on Route 160 for 16.9 miles to Isleton. Shortly beyond Isleton, Route 160 crosses the Sacramento River, but stay on the southeast bank, which is Isleton Road, to Walnut Grove, 9.3 miles beyond Isleton. Locke is .6 of a mile north of Walnut Grove. Both Isleton and Walnut Grove are interesting communities also worthy of your inspection.

Drawbridge

Certainly one of California's—or the West's, for that matter—most unusual ghost towns is Drawbridge. Created by the South Pacific Coast Railway Company in

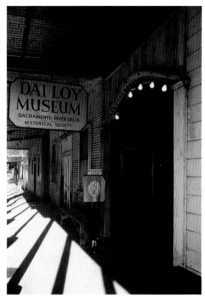

Both photos: The Dai Loy ("Big Welcome") Gambling Hall is now Locke's museum. In addition to historical photos, it features gaming tables, lottery baskets, and other gambling paraphernalia. The Dai Loy has a wonderful, dark, even mysterious mood about it.

1876 on Station Island, Drawbridge originally was merely a place where the railroad's bridge tender hand-cranked two drawbridges, which pivoted on central piers, to allow boats to pass through the railroad line.

The railroad traversed marshland that was a fishing and duck-hunting paradise, and eventually word spread of its wonders. Drawbridge became a popular stop along the railway, and by the turn of the twentieth century, a cottage industry of several gun clubs and two hotels had developed, along with as many as ninety residences, all built on stilts. It was common for 500 hunters to invade Drawbridge for a weekend during duck season.

With Prohibition, Drawbridge saw increased popularity as a place to gamble and quench one's thirst with homemade beer, wine, and whiskey. The town was close enough to a population center to be easily reached yet restricted enough in access to be easily guarded. It also conveniently lacked a police department.

The beginning of the Depression and the end of Prohibition decreased the hunting and fishing traffic, but Drawbridge was doomed when burgeoning nearby communities pumped fresh water from beneath the marshes, causing Station Island to begin sinking. In addition, those same towns dumped their raw sewage into the bay, which overwhelmed the bay's natural ability to dilute and filter it, making Drawbridge considerably less attractive. Finally, salt ponds constructed nearby closed out the tides around Station Island. By the 1950s, Drawbridge was largely deserted, although the last resident stayed until 1979.

Ironically, the wildfowl that brought hunters now have the run of the place: Drawbridge is part of an environmental education center and a wildlife sanctuary.

When You Go

At this writing, access to Drawbridge is closed. For information, check with the Don Edwards San Francisco Bay National Wildlife Refuge. Its visitors' center is located south of Thornton Avenue, the last exit heading west on State Route 84 before the Dumbarton Bridge crosses the bay. Signs lead you to the center, open from 10 A.M. to 5 P.M. every day except Monday and holidays. The visitors' center, naturally, emphasizes the refuge's wildlife, but it also has a display about Drawbridge, sells a highly informative booklet about the town, and offers a slide show on Drawbridge four times a year.

New Almaden

New Almaden, now a quiet refuge from expanding Silicon Valley, once had a remarkably crucial effect upon the history of the Gold Rush, California, and the United States of America. That is no exaggeration.

The Ohlone Indians used the reddish cinnabar, a form of mercuric sulfide, for personal decoration and paint, but when the Spanish found that same cinnabar in 1824, they knew its real value and began mining operations. This venture was the first quicksilver mine in North America and the first mine of any kind in California.

In 1845, major mining began. Originally the claim was known as the Santa Clara Mine or Chaboya's Mine, but it was known as New Almaden after 1848. The name

All photos: *The approximately two dozen deteriorating wooden buildings of Drawbridge are slowly sinking into a slough. No attempt is being made to preserve them.*

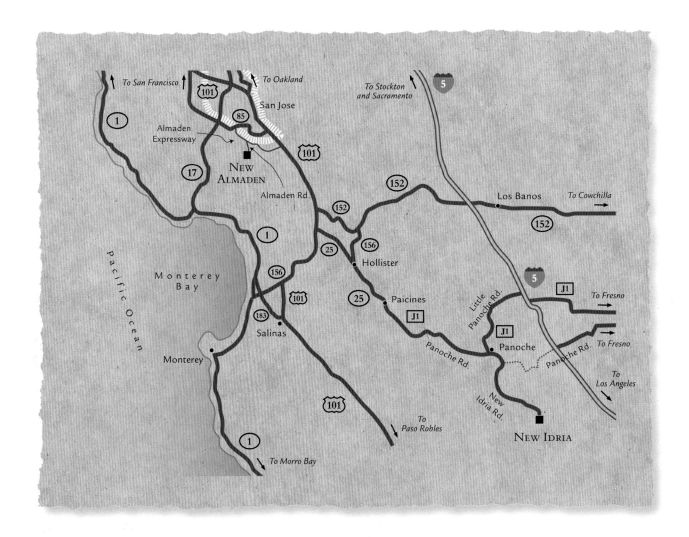

was in honor of Spain's Almaden Mine, which has supplied Europe with mercury for more than 2,000 years and is still producing today. California's Almaden produced more than a million flasks of quicksilver worth more than $70 million. The New Almaden Mine was the greatest producer of wealth of any single mine in California, gold or otherwise.

As impressive as those facts are, there is more to it than that. Mercury, called quicksilver because of its liquid mobility at ordinary temperatures, was essential until the 1880s as a prerequisite ingredient in the reduction of gold and silver. Until the discovery of the New Almaden deposits, the world's supply of mercury was controlled by a monopoly run by the English branch of the Rothschild family. The discovery at New Almaden, which, in a remarkable piece of timing, preceded the California Gold Rush by two years, freed California's incredible gold deposits from dependence upon foreign reduction materials and, as a result, foreign capital and influence. Because of New Almaden, California's gold—the richest concentration in the earth's history—was controlled by American—not European—capital.

Walking, Bicycling, and Horseback Riding Around New Almaden

Your first stop in New Almaden is Casa Grande, a twenty-room, two-story brick mansion built in 1854 that currently houses a mining museum whose emphasis is, naturally, on mercury. The displays give a veritable education on the methods of mining and uses of quicksilver. I suggest you park—and leave—your car there.

Available free at the museum is a brochure for a delightful town walking tour. Walk rather than drive the route because many buildings, which date from as early as the 1860s, feature informative historical plaques.

One stop on the tour is the Hacienda Cemetery. When Bertram Road bisected the preexisting cemetery, some graves were likely covered over. The road was named for Bertram Barrett, whose arm, but not his body, is buried there. Barrett lost his arm in 1898 at age thirteen in a hunting accident, and a law required it be buried. Barrett lived until 1959, and the rest of him is interred in San Jose.

To this point, the only evidence that this was a mining

New Almaden's Casa Grande was supposed to be a hotel, but instead it became the mine manager's elegant mansion. It now serves as a museum.

One stop along New Almaden's walking tour is the 1899 St. Anthony's Catholic Church, constructed to honor a promise by a New Almaden mother who prayed for the safe return of her son Antonio from the Spanish-American War.

town is found in the museum. But at the southwest end of town is Almaden Quicksilver County Park. Closed to motorized vehicles, the park is a delight for hikers, equestrians, and mountain bikers. It contains a different glimpse of New Almaden's history, because the park includes Mine Hill—the site of Spanish Camp and English Town, where 1,800 people lived.

I highly recommend exploring the park if you are able. A brochure with a detailed map is available at the entrance. Among the many remnants on the hill are the tall brick stack of the reduction works, the English Town schoolhouse, and a superb brick powderhouse. Assorted dumps, shafts, and foundations dot the area. The attractive Hidalgo Cemetery, with its Italian cypress trees, is the southernmost attraction. In all, I spent more than two hours riding a mountain bike around the old workings. If you walk, plan for considerably longer.

When You Go

From Sate Route 85 (the freeway on San Jose's southern end), take the Almaden Expressway exit and go south for 4 miles. Turn right on Almaden Road and follow it for 2.3 miles to New Almaden.

A primary attraction on the hill of Almaden Quicksilver Park is the reduction works, which stands near the entrance to the Hacienda Mine.

The mill and smelter at New Idria produced the second-largest amount of quicksilver in the United States, second only to New Almaden.

New Idria

If you are one of the millions who have driven endless Interstate 5 from Sacramento to Los Angeles, you may have looked west at the Diablo Range and wondered what on earth could be up there. Here is a partial answer: lovely, grass-covered rolling hills, plenty of cattle, and one interesting ghost town. New Idria, like New Almaden (see preceding entry), was a quicksilver town, located eighty-two miles southeast of New Almaden—if you could use the direct-flight feet of winged Mercury himself.

A cinnabar deposit discovered in 1853 created the New Idria Mine, named in honor of Idria, a famous Austrian quicksilver center. New Idria became California's second-largest producer of mercury after New Almaden. The town near the New Idria Mine took the mine's name when the post office was established in 1869; the postal service shortened the name to Idria in 1894. Residents, however, continued to call the community New Idria. There is also a disagreement about pronunciation: *California Place Names* gives "*id*-ri-uh," but residents have always said "*eye*-dree-uh."

Regardless of name or pronunciation, this is an interesting ghost town. Scrub brush and grass surround over two dozen buildings. Towering over the town is the mill and smelter, a large tin structure with a huge concrete base. The other buildings in town are wooden and painted gray or tan. The best is a two-story hotel, but also prominent are a combination dance hall and movie theater (now with a sign saying "General Store"), a mine rescue station, the post office, and several residences, including one on a hill above town that was formerly the school. The entire company town once had a population of about 500, primarily Mexican and Basque.

When I first visited in 1983, volunteers were mowing and hacking grass and weeds around the vacant buildings, because fire is a recurring threat. On my second visit in 1995, the town was being leased as a drug and alcohol rehabilitation center. When I returned in 2000, New Idria had a population of three people—and thirty dogs.

The road bisecting New Idria climbs immediately to a point that affords an excellent panorama of the town and mine. That road continues into the mountains and provides some stark, remarkable scenery before descending into the Clear Creek Recreation Area, where it deteriorates considerably and eventually enters an area that contains hazardous asbestos.

When You Go

The easiest paved route to New Idria begins on Interstate 5. Take the Little Panoche Road–Shields Avenue exit, 23 miles south of State Route 152, which crosses I-5 en route to Los Banos. Follow Little Panoche Road west and then south for 20 miles, where it will intersect with Panoche Road. Turn left and go 3 miles to a right turn onto New Idria Road. The town is 20.8 miles from this intersection on a paved road that is often only dirt-road wide. The last .3 of a mile, although paved, has deteriorated, but I watched a station wagon make it into town.

Chapter Five

GHOSTS OF THE EASTERN SIERRA

Main photo: *When people picture a place as a "ghost town," they probably envision something like Bodie's Main Street. From left are the Dechambeau Hotel, the I.O.O.F. Hall (with the Bodie Athletic Club downstairs), the Miners Union Hall, the morgue, and the Boone Store and Warehouse.*

Inset photo: *Kerosene lanterns and a marginally wearable shoe reside in Bodie's firehouse.*

The Eastern Sierra contains some of the West's most spectacular scenery. The eastern slopes of the Sierra Nevada (Spanish for "snow-covered range") are far more rugged than its western slopes, and the high desert below the mountains has a desolate beauty. Combine that with eerie, splendid Mono Lake and gorgeous Yosemite National Park, and you have a superb back-country destination.

But there's more. The area features the West's best ghost town as well. Now a state historic park, Bodie is the country's most extensive, best-preserved mining camp. In addition to Bodie, three minor true ghost towns—Masonic, Bennettville, and Mono Pass—reside in isolated, scenic splendor.

One important caveat about visiting these sites: Mono County's weather can quickly go from glorious to severe. Summer affords the best opportunity to see these ghost towns. Bodie, at an elevation of 8,375 feet, has ten to twenty feet of snow in the winter. Masonic is on a lonely back road. Bennettville and Mono Pass require hiking high into the back country. Make proper preparations and inquire locally about the weather.

Bodie

Bodie is absolutely unique. No ghost town has as much remaining from its heyday, and no place is maintained like Bodie. Now a state park, it is kept in a state of "arrested decay," which means that it is not being restored to its original condition but rather preserved in its present shape. When shingles or windows need replacement, they are identical to the original. Many buildings that have a charming lean are actually braced from within by specially trained carpenters.

And what buildings they are! Almost 170 remain, most of them made of wind-battered and sun-bleached wood. Although the majority are residences, Bodie also features a variety of commercial and mining-related structures. As many buildings as there are, they represent only one in twenty of Bodie's total number, as fires in 1892 and 1932 ravaged the town.

Although Bodie is a state park, it does not feel like one, because there are no tourist concession stands, no multi-media presentations, and no modern automobiles. There are also no food stands, so bring your own fare to eat. And you will need sustenance, because you will want to spend at least three hours in Bodie, and if you hope to see most of it, I recommend staying all day. I have visited more than 500 ghost towns in twelve states, and this one is the best.

Only four years after the discovery of gold, the Mother Lode was saturated with Argonauts. Late entrants found little opportunity for success and so ventured elsewhere. One of those disappointed prospectors was Waterman (or William—accounts differ) S. Body (also spelled "Bodey"), who came from Sonora to the Eastern Sierra after gold was discovered in Mono County in 1857. In

Prospectors of the Eastern Sierra often looked for quartz outcroppings in their search for primary gold deposits. This native gold on quartz shows why.

134

Perhaps as a comfort for grieving relatives, Bodie's morgue has an illustration, crudely framed, of a woman giving a look of pensive sympathy.

A dusty place setting graces the dining table at Lester Bell's house. Bell was the man in charge of Bodie's cyanide plant, the largest such operation in the country at the time.

1859, Body and a partner, E. S. "Black" Taylor, headed into the hills and found gold in Taylor Gulch, named for the partner, where they built a cabin.

Body, from Poughkeepsie, New York, never saw the glory of their discovery, as he died the next year in a snowstorm while bringing supplies to the cabin.

A mining district, including Taylor Gulch, was formed on July 10, 1860. The first recorded spelling of the camp as "Bodie" appeared in October 1862. Emil Billeb, a Bodie resident for decades, says the name was spelled that way because of a careless sign painter, but others claim it was a deliberate change because, spelled "Body," people were pronouncing it "*bah*-dee," not "*boh*-dee."

During the 1860s, Bodie enjoyed only modest prosperity, partly because of gold strikes across the Nevada border at Aurora, which boomed from 1861 until 1869. But Bodie's turn came when out-of-work Aurora and Virginia City miners reexamined Bodie Bluff.

The bonanza began in 1874, and two years later a cave-in at the Bunker Hill Mine exposed a rich concentration of gold ore. In 1878, a huge strike at the Bodie Mine brought a million dollars' worth of ore in only six weeks. In that year, Bodie's population reached about 3,000 people. Two years later, the population had more than tripled.

Building a metropolis at an elevation of more than 8,000 feet was no simple matter. The Bodie area is virtually treeless. Lumber for buildings and wood for fuel were freighted from a forest thirty-two miles away, south of Mono Lake, creating a lumber boom town called Mono Mills. In 1881, a narrow-gauge railroad from Mono Mills to Bodie made wood shipments cheaper and more reliable. It was a good thing, too, because Bodie's mines and mills consumed 45,000 cords of wood annually. (To visit the almost vanished site of Mono Mills, take U.S. 395 south from Lee Vining for 5 miles to State Route 120. Turn east and proceed 9.1 miles. An historic plaque, one concrete foundation, pinkish stone blocks, and scattered timber remain.)

Mono Mills's lumber created a boisterous Bodie, with sixty-five saloons and gambling halls, seven breweries, and a red-light district on Bonanza Street, which was

Overleaf: The Bodie Cemetery is an excellent place from which to view a panorama of the historic town. The most identifiable building in town is the 1882 Methodist Church. On Bodie Bluff (far right) is the Standard Mill.

facetiously known as Maiden Lane or Virgin Alley. The jail was conveniently located immediately east of Bonanza. A minister in 1881 proclaimed the place "a sea of sin, lashed by the tempests of lust and passion."

A "sea of sin" is naturally going to have its share of violence as well. Bodie became notorious for its shootings and murders, and citizens were so accustomed to the mayhem that a corpse discovered in the morning was known as "a man for breakfast."

But that is only one version of Bodie. Popular histories tend to emphasize, even glorify, the violent and tempestuous nature of bonanza camps, as if drunken, bawdy, murderous behavior was both accepted and the norm. It was neither. Grant H. Smith, later a respected mining attorney, came to Bodie at age fourteen in 1879 and served as a telegraph messenger boy. As a result, he entered every imaginable social and business situation. He counters Bodie's scurrilous reputation, saying, "These men, as a rule, were virile, enthusiastic, and free-living, bound by very few of the rules of conventional society. However, they had an admirable code of ethics: liberal-minded, generous to a fault, square-dealing, and completely devoid of pretense and hypocrisy. . . . A friend in Bodie was a friend for life."

But Bodie's reputation, Smith's efforts notwithstanding, will forever be tainted toward its lawless side by one famous quote, uttered by a little girl whose family was moving from Aurora to the infamous town. In her evening prayer, she was overheard by her parents saying, "Goodbye, God, I'm going to Bodie." Aurora journalists used the prayer to ridicule Bodie, but Bodie journalists, in a rejoinder, insisted that the tone and punctuation were vastly different. What the little girl had actually said was "Good! By God, I'm going to Bodie!"

Bodie's boom times lasted a mere three years. During its peak, almost fifty mines were producing ore that was fed to ten mills with a combined 162 stamps. By 1882, however, the population had dropped drastically from about 10,000 to less than 500. In 1883, Bodie mine stocks

The Boone Store and Warehouse holds a true mystery: State park officials cannot open the safe, and no one knows what is inside.

crashed. The town was virtually lifeless.

During the bonanza years, an estimated $21 million in gold had been extracted. Naturally, some refused to believe that Bodie's glory days were over, and one of those became the person crucial to Bodie's present-day state of preservation—James Stuart Cain.

Jim Cain came from Canada in 1875 at age twenty-one looking to find his fortune in Carson City, Nevada, just when the Comstock Lode was in decline. Like many others, he went to Bodie, arriving in 1879.

Cain began in the lumber and freighting business. As Bodie boomed, he supplied much of the wood, transporting it across Mono Lake by barge. As he prospered, he diversified by investing in mines and leasing the Bodie Railroad and Lumber Company, which replaced his barge. When Bodie's fortunes plummeted, Cain stayed, buying bargain-rate mines and the Bodie Bank.

In 1890, Cain brought to Bodie the then-new cya-

Also inside the Boone Store and Warehouse are a dressmaker's fitting form and two calendars, one from Los Angeles and the other from Bridgeport, the seat of Mono County.

nide process to treat previously worthless tailings. To lower costs at the highly successful cyanide plants, he brought electric power to Bodie, the first use of electricity generated over long-distance lines (the hydroelectric plant was thirteen miles away). The technology was so untested that power lines were laid in a straight line, for fear that if the line curved, the electricity might jump off into space.

The successful use of long-distance electricity at Bodie caused a revolution in the way mines were powered and changed the way the world produced ore.

The cyanide tailings process kept Bodie profitable into the early twentieth century, but Cain was convinced that Bodie would have another windfall from new gold deposits.

One constant in all these dealings was Cain's Bodie Bank. Although he was a banker, Cain hardly fit the stereotype. His bank, for example, had calendars, featuring pin-up girls, on the walls.

Moreover, Cain was known for his practical jokes. His bank had one of Bodie's earliest telephones, and a Chinese businessman (after being convinced that the phone could "speak" Chinese as well as English) often used it to call the Wells Fargo agent in Hawthorne, Nevada, for an update on his produce order. He invariably inquired about sweet potatoes, so Cain called the agent in advance to alert him and then placed three sweet potatoes in the phone's battery box. When the gentleman inquired about sweet potatoes, the agent informed him he would send them immediately by wire. Cain then ceremoniously opened the battery box, and the sweet potatoes dropped to the floor. The stupefied grocer requested that the entire order be sent by wire.

Cain operated the bank for forty years, until 1932. He would open every weekday at 10 A.M. to no customers. In that year, a boy playing with matches started a fire that leveled about two-thirds of Bodie's largely vacant

A leaning picket fence runs beside the home of Theodore Hoover, the general manager of the Standard Consolidated Mine Company. The brother of Herbert Hoover, he later became Director of the School of Mines at Stanford University.

business district. The fire consumed Cain's bank, although the vault held and the safe inside protected its contents. In that same year, Cain left Bodie for good, moving to San Francisco, where he died in 1939 at age eighty-five.

But Cain's legacy did not die. He had the foresight to hire a watchman to protect the town, and in 1962 Bodie became a state park. Because of Jim Cain, Bodie stands as a monument to the rush for riches in the American West.

Walking Around Bodie

The brochure you receive when you enter Bodie suggests a logical walking tour. Remember to peer into every building through as many windows as you can to study its contents.

For example, if you gaze into the living room window of the Metzger House on Fuller Street, you will see a dusty old doll carriage, a wooden sled, and a small toy dog for a child to sit on and rock, like a hobby horse.

In Sam Leon's Bar on Main Street, you squint into the semidarkness to make out roulette tables, a bar, a one-armed bandit, and gaming tables stacked with chips as if waiting for the next hand.

A comment I have heard several times on my Bodie visits is that it is unfortunate that we can only gaze through the windows of most buildings. But if we could step inside, floors would have to be reinforced, valuable objects would have to be placed out of reach, and the whole feeling of Bodie—that people up and left in a moment—would be seriously compromised. The town is much more genuine because we cannot enter most structures.

In the center of town, on Main Street south of Green Street, stands the 1878 Miners Union Hall, which houses the park's interesting museum. While in the hall, consider purchasing tickets to one of the park's outstanding tours.

The most frequently offered tour is of the huge 1899 Standard Mill, east of town on the slopes of Bodie Bluff.

Tattered curtains and an ownerless hat give this window scene in Bodie a look of true abandonment. The house once was the residence of Pat Reddy, a one-armed criminal lawyer well known in Bodie.

Someone was counting on the queen of diamonds in this long-forgotten card game at Sam Leon's Bar.

Above: *Textbooks, student assignments, and even a teacher's hat give the impression that everyone simply left class at the Bodie Schoolhouse and never came back. Note the festive Easter bunnies on the walls.*

Right: *A prosperous Bodie had its share of Fourth of July and other celebratory parades, as this stack of flags attests. Proper flag etiquette, however, did not seem to be a concern, as these are merely piled in the corner of the second floor of the schoolhouse. A child's stroller holds several flags.*

Tours are given as if you were a 1905 prospective employee, a delightful illusion that makes the experience more genuine.

Two other tours go into otherwise closed-off areas, including mine shafts and the train depot. They do not run daily, however, and are given but once a day even when offered, so inquire before you visit.

The 1879 Bodie Schoolhouse, on Green east of Main, offers one of the most fascinating glances into Bodie's past. Originally the Bon Ton Lodging House, the building was pressed into educational service when a delinquent burned down the first school. When you peer through the windows, notice textbooks on desks and a wooden globe whose maps have peeled off, leaving it merely a large wooden ball. A wall clock, appropriately, has no hands.

Bodie's cemetery (actually three adjoining graveyards) is .3 of a mile southwest of town. The site is well worth exploring, and not just because of its many interesting headstones. It also affords a sweeping view of Bodie. An informative cemetery guide is available at the gate for purchase or loan.

Two of the most beautifully carved headstones I have ever seen stand in the Bodie cemetery. One, for James B. Perry, looks like quarried rock, but from it evolves a graceful, curving parchment from which we learn that Perry died in 1896 at sixty-three years of age and served as a Mono County supervisor. A similar marker, certainly crafted by the same stonemason, stands nearby for Danish native Annie C. Fouke.

One story that the cemetery guide does not tell is about the now-missing Pagdin family headstone. It was made of hollow iron, with detachable bolts holding the front and rear plates. During Prohibition, a customer would remove the bolts and leave money. A bootlegger would slide to the cemetery and leave a cache of liquor. As longtime resident Emil Billeb put it, "After Repeal there were noticeably fewer mourners visiting the cemetery."

After you have completed your tour of Bodie, you might recall those journalists who doctored the little Aurora girl's prayer. In a way, they were speaking for present-day ghost town enthusiasts—Bodie has become our mecca, and now we can justifiably say, "Good! By God, I'm going to Bodie!"

When You Go

From Lee Vining, drive 18 miles north on U.S. 395. Turn east on State Route 270 and proceed 12.3 miles to the state park. All but the last 2.7 miles are paved. In good weather, even motor homes traverse the route.

Masonic

After Bodie, anything is going to be an anticlimax. But the backroads drive between Bodie and Masonic is lovely, and Masonic's townsite is more representative of a true California ghost town.

The Masonic Mining District was formed in 1862 by Masons from Aurora, Nevada, who found modest gold-producing ores. The claims were largely abandoned when huge strikes were found back in Aurora.

In about 1900, an excited Joe Green staked the rich—and appropriately named—Jump Up Joe Mine. On the Fourth of July, 1902, Pennsylvanian J. S. Phillips and two partners made a strike and called it the Pittsburg-Liberty, commemorating Phillips's birthplace (but somehow misplacing the final "h") and the date of discovery.

Ruins of a stone miner's cabin sit among the boulders of Masonic.

Above: *Shingling and metal sheeting of varied eras confirm that someone worked diligently to keep this shed at the Chemung Mine in service in a harsh land.*

Right: *The Chemung Mine still has its ore sorter (left), remnants of a headframe (center), and its mill (right).*

The town took the name of the mining district, and by 1906 Masonic had a new post office, hotel, three grocery stores, and a population of about 500. One thing it lacked, ironically, was a Masonic lodge. The town had three sections—Upper Town, Middle Town, and Lower Town—about a half-mile from each other.

The principal mine was the Pittsburg-Liberty, which operated until 1910 and yielded approximately $700,000 in gold. By 1911, Masonic was dying, although some mines were reworked in the 1920s.

When you arrive at a junction 15.2 miles northwest of Bodie, you actually will be nearest to the Upper Town of Masonic, but nothing remains. Turn right and proceed north to see the best remnants. A hopper will appear on the left, followed by rubble on the right, the only evidence of Middle Town, which once had the office of the town's newspaper, *The Masonic Pioneer*, and Boone and Son's mercantile, whose main store was in Bodie.

Continue to Lower Town, where you will find a stone house, with roof beams collapsing into the interior; a commemorative plaque; and a log cabin with roof beams but no roof.

Beyond the cabins is Masonic's most impressive remnant, the Pittsburg-Liberty Mill and Cyanide Plant. Its ten stamps have been salvaged and the building is a mere foundation, but it is impressive nonetheless. Note how effectively the mill's builders used the hillside's rock as part of the foundation.

Beyond the mill are two log cabin ruins, with scattered tin rubble, and stone foundations.

The Chemung Mine, which operated from 1909

Above: *A mine adit stands west of Bennettville. When I was last there, chilly water was flowing out of the mine opening. In addition, I smelled a strong animal odor emanating from the tunnel, which made me a little leery about who might currently inhabit it.*

Left: *Bennettville's first-story stable and second-story bunkhouse is the larger of the town's two standing buildings.*

until about 1938, is southwest of Masonic on the road to Bridgeport. The Chemung consists of six wooden structures, all more or less under roof.

When You Go

If you have a truck: From Bodie, take the Bodie-Masonic Road (originally the Geiger Grade), which heads west from Bodie's parking lot. Look back within the first 1.3 miles for excellent panoramas of Bodie. In 8.6 miles, Aurora Canyon Road goes left. Your road continues northwest. At this writing, a sign painted on a large rock points the way. Drive another 6.6 miles to a junction and turn right. The main ruins of Masonic occur in one mile. To see the Chemung Mine, return the one mile to the junction, turn right, and proceed for 2.8 miles. That road continues on to Bridgeport.

If you have a passenger car: From Bodie, return to U.S. 395. Turn right and go 6.3 miles north to the outskirts of Bridgeport. Turn right onto State Route 182 and proceed north for 3.8 miles. Turn right onto Masonic Road. The Chemung Mine will be on your right in 5.1 miles. In 2.8 miles beyond the Chemung, you will come to a junction. Turn left and go one mile to Masonic's principal ruins.

Bennettville

Bennettville and Mono Pass (see the following entry) contain such sparse ruins that many readers of this book may decide to overlook the sites. Don't be one of them.

Bennettville (also known as Tioga) stands in beautiful isolation, feeling far more than a mere mile from civilization. The short twenty-minute hike to the site crosses a small brook and passes next to Mine Creek as it dramatically cascades through a narrow canyon.

Two plaques about Bennettville, one at the Saddlebag Lake turnoff and another at the Tioga Lake Overlook, imply the town has completely vanished. Bennettville, however, still has two of its original fourteen buildings perched on a rocky hill waiting for the photographer or artist.

The Sheepherder Mine, located in 1874, preceded Bennettville. It was named because a shepherd found a rusty pick and shovel from an old working known as the Thundering Big Silver Ledge of Tioga Hill. The town that grew at the site between 1882 and 1884 was named for Thomas Bennett Jr., president of the Great Sierra Silver Mining Company.

You have heard of mining towns going "from boom to bust." This one was simply a bust. Despite transporting eight tons of equipment and spending $300,000 of shareholders' money, not one shipment of ore was ever made. By 1890 Bennettville was a ghost town.

More than a hundred years later, Bennettville consists of an assay office and a two-story stable and bunkhouse, both restored in 1993.

Readers of this book certainly know not to remove anything from an historic site like Bennettville. On my most recent visit, a collection of relics sat on a flat-topped boulder near the buildings: tin cans, a piece of bed frame, pottery remnants, broken glass, and nails. The unwritten message was simple: This reflects what remains of this site. It is all worthless. Look at it, pick it up, but leave it for others to enjoy.

A mine adit, less than two-tenths of a mile away, is clearly visible southwest of Bennettville. If you wish to walk over, take the trail that goes from the assay office off to the northwest, because that trail offers a log crossing of Mine Creek.

At the adit itself are remnants of two boilers, a two-cylinder engine, and a geared apparatus with an embossment stating that it is a Baker's Rotary Pressure Blower, patented in 1873 and built in Philadelphia.

Despite the fact that Bennettville was a complete failure, the mining district did have one very positive effect on the area: To get that eight tons of equipment into Bennettville, a road across Tioga Pass from the west was constructed at a cost of $60,000. It now is the highway from western Yosemite National Park to Tuolumne Meadows and beyond.

When You Go

Drive south from Lee Vining .5 of a mile and turn right on State Route 120, the road to Yosemite National Park's eastern entrance. Take Route 120 for 10 miles to the turnoff to Saddlebag Lake and turn right. The trailhead to Bennettville is 200 feet to the west, near the campground host's space. Bennettville is less than a half mile away as the eagle flies, but almost a mile on the ground.

Mono Pass

Mono Pass consists of five white bark log cabins, a waste dump, a water-filled shaft—and an astonishing view. The seven-mile round-trip hike to visit the site is enchanting—if you are in appropriate condition. As your walk begins at 9,697 feet elevation and will climb to 10,604 feet, this is not a casual stroll.

Famed naturalist John Muir crossed Mono Pass in 1869. He wrote that the trail was made popular in 1858 as a route to the Mono gold excitement but that it had been used by animals, Indians, and mountain men long before that. The route was ignored, however, after the road over Tioga Pass was constructed to Bennettville in the early 1880s.

The cabins and debris at Mono Pass also date from

Above and overleaf: *The cabins at Mono Pass stand at 10,604 feet elevation, by far the highest in this book. They housed miners for the Ella Boss and Golden Crown gold mines.*

the 1880s. The Koip Peak topographic map shows four mine shafts and one "prospect." Judging from the small waste dumps at the site, I suspect very little ore was actually extracted.

When You Go

From the Bennettville trailhead, drive west on State Route 120 for about 2 miles to Tioga Pass, the entrance to Yosemite National Park. The daily entrance fee is not inexpensive, and you might question the cost solely for a hike to a minor ghost town. My advice is simple—while there, venture farther into Yosemite.

The trailhead to Mono Pass is in Dana Meadow, 1.5 miles beyond the park entrance on the southeast side of the road.

Note: An alternate route to Mono Pass, one I have not taken, begins at Walker Lake on the eastern side of the Sierra Nevada and climbs for six miles to Mono Pass. A Forest Service employee who has hiked both trails told me that, although lovely, the trail from Walker Lake is considerably steeper than the one from Dana Meadow. (John Muir says that Sierra passes climb about a thousand feet to the mile on the eastern side but a much tamer two hundred feet per mile from the west). Approaching from the east, however, saves you admission to Yosemite. For directions to Walker Lake, go to the U.S. Forest Service Information Center, a half mile north of Lee Vining on U.S. 395.

Glossary of Mining Terms

adit: A nearly horizontal entrance to a hardrock mine.

Argonauts: The men who came to California during the Gold Rush in search of riches.

arrastra: An apparatus used to grind ore by means of a heavy stone that is dragged around in a circle, normally by mules or oxen.

assay: To determine the value of a sample of ore, in ounces per ton, by testing using a chemical evaluation.

claim: A tract of land with defined boundaries that includes mineral rights extending downward from the surface.

diggings (or "diggins"): Evidence of mining efforts, such as placer, hydraulic, or dredge workings.

dredge: An apparatus, usually on a flat-bottomed boat, that scoops material out of a river to extract gold-bearing sand or gravel; used in "dredging" or "dredge mining."

dust: Minute gold particles found in placer deposits.

flume: An inclined, man-made channel, usually of wood, used to convey water or mine waste, often for long distances.

hardrock mining: The process in which a primary deposit (see page 153) is mined by removing ore-bearing rock by tunneling into the earth. Also known as quartz mining, since gold is frequently found in quartz deposits.

headframe: The vertical apparatus over a mine shaft that has cables to be lowered down the shaft for raising either ore or a cage; sometimes called a "gallows frame."

high-grading: The theft of rich ore, usually by a miner

The Kennedy Mine's headframe is the largest still standing in the Mother Lode. A wheel at the top of the apparatus would help cables (now missing) pull ore and miners out of the vertical shaft, which was almost 6,000 feet deep, at the headframe's base. Ore would be dropped into the chutes of the ore sorter (right).

working for someone else who owns the mine.

hydraulic mining: A method of mining using powerful jets of water to wash away a bank of gold-bearing earth (see especially Malakoff Diggins, chapter two). Also known by miners as "hydraulicking."

ingot: A cast bar or block of a metal.

lode: A continuous mineral-bearing deposit or vein (see also "Mother Lode," below).

mill: A building in which rock is crushed to extract minerals by one of several methods. If this is done by stamps (heavy hammers or pestles), it is a stamp mill. If by iron balls, it is a ball mill. The mill is usually constructed on the side of a hill to utilize its slope, hence, a "gravity-fed mill."

mining district: An area of land described (usually for legal purposes) and designated as containing valuable minerals in paying amounts.

monitor: The nozzle, somewhat like a water cannon, used in hydraulicking; also called a "giant."

Mother Lode: The principal lode passing through a district or section of the country; from the same term in Spanish, "La Veta Madre." In California, it refers to the hundred-mile-long concentration of gold on the western slopes of the Sierra Nevada.

nugget: A lump of native gold or other mineral. The largest found in the Mother Lode weighed 195 pounds.

ore: A mineral of sufficient concentration, quantity, and value to be mined at a profit.

ore sorter: A structure, usually near a mine, in which higher-grade ore is sorted from lower-grade ore or waste before being sent to the mill or smelter (see photo, facing page).

pan: To look for placer gold by washing earth, gravel, or sand, usually in a stream bed.

placer: A waterborne deposit of sand or gravel containing heavier materials like gold, which have been eroded from their original bedrock and concentrated as small particles that can be washed, or "panned," out (see also "secondary deposit," below).

pocket: In primary deposits, a small but rich concentration of gold embedded in quartz. In secondary deposits, a hole or indentation in a stream bed in which gold dust or nuggets have been trapped.

powderhouse: A structure placed safely away from a mine that stored such volatile materials as gun powder and dynamite. The building's walls are usually very stout, but its roof is intentionally of flimsier construction, so if the contents should explode, the main force of the blast would be into the air.

primary deposit: A deposit of gold or other mineral found in its original location. Ore is extracted by hardrock mining or hydraulic mining.

prospect: Mineral workings of unproven value.

quartz mining: See "hardrock mining," above.

salting: To place valuable minerals in a place in which they do not actually occur. Done to deceive.

secondary deposit: A deposit of gold or other mineral that has been moved from its original location by water. Ore is extracted by placer mining or dredging.

shaft: A vertical or nearly vertical opening into the earth for hardrock mining.

slag: The waste product of a smelter; hence, slag dumps.

smelter: A building or complex in which material is melted in order to separate impurities from pure metal.

strike: The discovery of a primary or secondary deposit of gold or other mineral in sufficient concentration and/or quantity to be mined profitably.

tailings: Waste or refuse left after milling is complete; sometimes used more generally, although incorrectly, to indicate waste dumps.

tramway: An apparatus for moving materials such as ore, rock, or even supplies in buckets suspended from pulleys that run on a cable.

waste dump: Waste rock, not of sufficient value to warrant milling, that comes out of a mine; usually found immediately outside a mine's entrance.

workings: A general term indicating any mining development; when that development is exhausted, it is "worked out."

Bibliography

Arizona Daily Star, 22 December 1985; 16 September 1990; 30 November 1997.

Bailey, Lynn R. *Supplying the Mining World.* Tucson, Arizona: Westernlore Press, 1996.

Beck, Warren A., and Ynez D. Haase. *Historical Atlas of California.* Norman: University of Oklahoma Press, 1974.

Billeb, Emil W. *Mining Camp Days.* Las Vegas: Nevada Publications, 1968.

Branding Iron, number 183. Los Angeles: Publication of The Westerners, Los Angeles Corral, Spring 1991.

Brewer, William H. *Up and Down California.* New Haven: Yale University Press, 1974.

Bruff, Joseph Goldsborough. *Gold Rush.* New York: Columbia University Press, 1949.

Cain, Ella M. *The Story of Bodie.* San Francisco: Fearon Publishers, 1956.

California Geology, February 1982; April 1982; June 1982; November 1982; March 1983; May 1983; March 1984; March 1987.

California Historical Landmarks. Sacramento: Department of Recreation, State of California, 1979, rev. 1981.

California Historical Quarterly. volumes 14, 26, 54, 56, 66, 67.

Carter, William. *Ghost Towns of the West:* Menlo Park, California: Lane Magazine and Book Company, 1971 and 1978.

Caughey, John. *Gold is the Cornerstone.* Berkeley: University of California Press, 1948.

Chalfant, W. A. *Gold, Guns and Ghost Towns.* Stanford: Stanford University Press, 1947.

Collier's, 6 August 1954.

Chidsey, D. B. *The California Gold Rush.* New York: Crown Publishers, 1968.

Dewey, O. L. "Monty." *Drawbridge, California: A Hand-Me-Down History.* Fremont, California: San Francisco Bay Wildlife Society, 1989.

Dillon, Richard H. *Exploring the Mother Lode Country.* Pasadena: Ward Ritchie Press, 1974.

Discovering Locke, n.d.

Frontier Times, August 1985.

Gillenkirk, Jeff, and James Motlow. *Bitter Melon.* Berkeley: Heyday Books, 1987.

Gold Rush Country. Menlo Park, California: Lane Books, 1968.

Gudde, Erwin G. *California Gold Camps.* Berkeley: University of California Press, 1975.

——————. *California Place Names* (third edition). Berkeley: University of California Press, 1969.

Hill, Mary. *Gold: The California Story.* Berkeley: University of California Press, 1999.

Holliday, J. S. *The World Rushed In.* New York: Simon & Schuster, 1981.

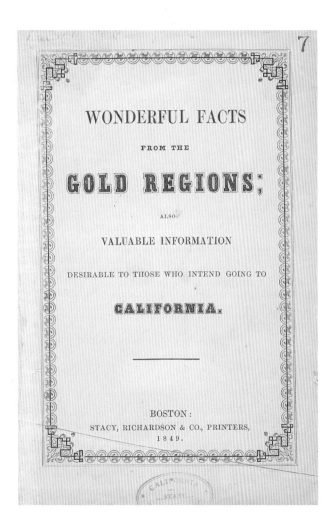

7

WONDERFUL FACTS

FROM THE

GOLD REGIONS;

ALSO

VALUABLE INFORMATION

DESIRABLE TO THOSE WHO INTEND GOING TO

CALIFORNIA.

BOSTON:
STACY, RICHARDSON & CO., PRINTERS,
1849.

This enticing 1849 pamphlet, touting its "well-authenticated facts from the Gold Regions," also warned that other such publications contained inaccurate reports. (California State Library, California History Room)

Hoover, Mildred Brooke; Hero Eugene Rensch; Ethel Grace Rensch; William N. Abeloe (revised by Douglas E. Kyle). *Historic Spots in California* (fourth edition). Stanford: Stanford University Press, 1990.

Hubbard, Douglass. *Ghost Mines of Yosemite*. Fresno: Awani Press, 1971.

Hulbert, Archer Butler. *Forty-Niners: The Chronicle of the California Trail*. Boston: Little, Brown, 1931.

Jackson, Joseph Henry. *Anybody's Gold: The Story of California's Mining Towns*. San Francisco: Chronicle Books, 1970.

——————— (editor). *Gold Rush Album*. New York: Charles Scribner's Sons, 1949.

Jenkins, Olaf P. (director). *Geologic Guidebook Along Highway 49– Sierran Gold Belt: The Mother Lode Country*. San Francisco: State of California, Division of Mines, 1948.

Jones, Alice Goen (editor). *Trinity County Historic Sites*. Weaverville, California: Trinity County Historical Society, 1981.

Leadabrand, Russ. *Exploring California Byways* (vol. V). Los Angeles: Ward Ritchie Press, 1971.

Los Angeles Times, 4 June 1989; 29 April, 1990; 1 July 1992.

Miller, Donald. *Ghost Towns of California*. Boulder, Colorado: Pruett Publishing Company, 1978.

Modoc Travel Loops , n.d.

Moore, Thomas. *Bodie: Ghost Town*. South Brunswick and New York: A. S. Barnes and Company, 1969.

Muir, John. *The Mountains of California*. Berkeley: Ten Speed Press, 1977 (reprint of 1898 edition).

Murbarger, Nell, *Ghosts of the Glory Trail*. Los Angeles: Westernlore Press, 1956.

Nadeau, Remi. *Ghost Towns and Mining Camps of California*. Los Angeles: Ward Ritchie Press, 1965.

Northern California Traveler, July 1996.

Paul, Rodman W. *California Gold: the Beginning of Mining in the Far West*. Cambridge, Massachusetts: Harvard University Press, 1947.

———————. *The California Gold Discovery*. Georgetown, California: Talisman Press, 1966.

Petrides, George A. *A Field Guide to Western Trees: Western United States and Canada*. New York: Houghton Mifflin, 1992.

Rolle, Andrew F. *California, A History*. New York: Crowell, 1998.

Roske, Ralph Joseph. *Everyman's Eden*. New York: MacMillan, 1968.

San Francisco Chronicle, 7 April 2000.

San Francisco Examiner, 4 August 1996; 11 August 1996.

Shaffer, Jeffrey P. *Yosemite National Park: A Natural History Guide to Yosemite and Its Trails* (fourth edition). Berkeley: Wilderness Press, 1999.

The American West, May/June 1976.

The Mother Lode. Los Angeles: Automobile Club of Southern California, 1982 and 1993 editions.

Toleman, Vera, and Hazel Davis, editors. *The Siskiyou Pioneer,* volume 3, number 9. Yreka, California: Siskiyou County Historical Society, 1966.

Watkins, T. H. *California, An Illustrated History*. Palo Alto: American West Publishing Co., 1973.

Williams, George III. *The Guide to Bodie and Eastern Sierra Historic Sites*. Riverside, California: Tree By the River Publishing, 1981.

Wolle, Muriel Sibell. *The Bonanza Trail*. Chicago: The Swallow Press, 1953.

Wood, Raymund F. (editor). *The Westerners Brand Book, #16*. Los Angeles: The Westerners, Los Angeles Corral, 1982.

Acknowledgments

Philip Varney

For assistance in historical research: Matthew S. Sugarman, Park Superintendent, Marshall Gold Discovery State Historic Park; Michael Amorosa, Black Diamond Mines Regional Preserve; Brad Swander, Public Information Office, Yosemite National Park; Elizabeth Braydis, Office Manager, Calaveras Historical Society; Richard Camarena, Tuolumne County Museum; Linda Spear, The Kennedy Mine Foundation; Buzz Baxter of Chinese Camp; Pat Barry and Laurie Stefenoni of Fort Bidwell; Barney Lusk of North San Juan; Nedra Kayner and Linda Failmezger, Tucson-Pima Public Library; Bill Broyles; Dennis Judstra; Kathy McNicholas; David F. Myrick; Bruce J. Dinges, Director of Publications, Arizona Historical Society; and, especially, Richard Dillon of Mill Valley, for bibliographical recommendations.

For field-work support: MaryAnn Mead; Diane Holland; Darrell and Joyce Oldridge; Janet Varney; John and Susan Drew; Jim Holland; Nancy Reed; Fred and Milly Hardie; Betty Rowe; John and Roberta Crawford; Don DeYoung; Mary Robinson; George Hovey; Freeman B. Hover; Joy Neverman; Beth Parker-Martin.

And, especially, for photography: John and Susan Drew. The expertise and creative eye of John and Susan Drew are evident on every page of this book. In addition, they have given me suggestions, encouragement, and even food and shelter. We three are a team in the truest and best sense of the word. If my text gives this book substance, it is their images that give it life.

John and Susan Drew

First and foremost, this book would not be what it is without the superb writing of Philip Varney; his writing is the meat and substance of the book. Not only is his writing excellent, but he is a delight to work with. We have formed a close friendship through our work on our ghost town books.

It seems that at every turn we found people who went out of their way to help us obtain photographs that bring life to the tales these old towns want to tell. Some that were particularly helpful were Drew Merry at the Almaden Quicksilver County Park; Carolyn Fregulia at the Kennedy Mine in Jackson; Ranger Shirley Mraz at Marshall Gold Discovery State Historic Park; Don Biagi at the Malakoff Diggins State Historic Park; Rod Peese and Fred Bunge at Smartville; Ranger Michael Whitehead at Angel Island State Park; Betty Foster at Drawbridge; Ranger Margee Hench at Alcatraz Island; John Crane at Pilot Hill; and Ranger Sherrin Grout at Columbia State Historic Park.

Above: Melting snow accentuates the La Porte Cemetery. The town's old schoolhouse stands beyond the graveyard fence.

Facing page: Smartville's Catholic church shows decades of neglect.

Index

About the Author and Photographers

Left to right: Philip Varney, Susan Drew, John Drew. (Photograph by Caryn Haman)

Philip Varney

Philip Varney was in high school when his family moved from Illinois to Arizona. He quickly became fascinated by the history of the West, especially when finding that history meant exploring scenic back roads. Today, he travels extensively, both by car and bicycle, in the western United States.

Ghost Towns of Northern California is his sixth book on ghost towns. In his previous books, he took readers to visit the ghost towns of Arizona, New Mexico, and Southern California. He first collaborated with photographer John Drew on *Ghost Towns of Colorado*, which was published by Voyageur Press in 1999. He is also the author of a book on bicycle tours in southern Arizona and is a regular contributor to *Arizona Highways* magazine.

He makes his home in Tucson.

John and Susan Drew

John and Susan Drew call Jackson Hole, Wyoming, home, but during the cold of winter they may be in California or other areas, exploring back roads for ghost towns and beautiful scenery.

John and Susan have thirty-five years of photographic experience between them. Their work as been published both nationally and internationally in calendars, magazines, and books, including *Ghost Towns of Colorado* (Voyageur Press, 1999) and the *Texas Wildflower Postcard Collection* (Voyageur Press, 1988).